STUCK

A COMPLETE GUIDE TO ANSWERING
TOUGH QUESTIONS
ABOUT ABORTION

JUSTINA VAN MANEN

Life Cycle Books

ISBN: 978-0-919225-58-9

Published & distributed by Life Cycle Books
www.lifecyclebooks.com   orders@lifecyclebooks.com

Printed in Canada

Cover & image design by Sharon Grisnich

Dedication

To all those who have stepped forward to fill their place in the pro-life movement and tirelessly work to defend precious pre-born children. On behalf of the millions of children who cannot speak for themselves: Thank you.

Table of Contents

Preface

The book you hold in your hands does not break any new ground in the abortion debate or present any brand-new arguments. Instead, what we at the Canadian Centre for Bio-Ethical Reform have sought to create is a *textbook*, one which draws from the books authored by pro-life apologists such as Scott Klusendorf, Randy Alcorn, and Stephanie Gray, and presents the pro-life arguments in a practical and comprehensive way. We truly believe that if every single person with pro-life convictions would learn a handful of simple pro-life arguments and could feel comfortable using them with his or her peers, we could be well on our way to rebuilding a pro-life culture.

As an educational pro-life organization facilitating tens of thousands of face-to-face conversations about abortion with pro-choice people every year, those of us at Canadian Centre for Bio-Ethical Reform believe this textbook will be an easy-to-read, easy-to-use, one-stop-shop for everything you need to know to have a conversation with your co-worker, friend, or fellow student about abortion. You don't need to be a full-time pro-life activist or apologist to change someone's mind about abortion. You only need to familiarize yourself with the arguments and discussion tactics that the pro-life movement has pioneered over the past five decades.

Stuck is a culmination of the hard work of pro-life apologists and street activists—and every single argument contained in this textbook has been used to change someone's mind from pro-choice to pro-life. We hope you will find it useful, and that you will use it to save lives.

—The Canadian Centre for Bio-Ethical Reform

Introduction

When I was a teenager, a friend asked me, "Sam, what would you say to a girl considering an abortion?"

I was honest with her. I told her, 'I don't know.' I was 18 at the time. I wasn't a Christian. I wasn't a critical thinker. And I didn't care about abortion. I thought she was asking a hypothetical question. I didn't know she was asking for help.

I didn't know she was pregnant. I didn't know she was being pressured by her boyfriend to get an abortion. I didn't know I could have saved a life with my answer. I didn't know that just a few days later, my friend would get an abortion.[1]
~ Samuel Sey

How many of us have stories like this? How many missed opportunities have resulted in the tragic loss of a child's life? Perhaps this seems far-fetched. Perhaps abortion has never appeared to touch us personally. Think again. Every day in North America, thousands of children are walked into clinics, where they are suctioned to pieces and torn apart by abortionists. Since the decriminalization of abortion, *70 million* children have gone missing. Never before has a tragedy of such magnitude taken place—never has there been such a devastating loss of life. Our culture is broken, and the number of people who have been touched by abortion is staggering. We meet them on the streets, in the workplace, in our churches, schools, and homes. They are our neighbours, our friends, our relatives. If we believe that abortion has never touched us or the people that we love, we are lying to ourselves.

---

1   Sey, Samuel. "Why I wasn't writing," *Slow to Write,* August 30, 2018. https://slowtowrite.com/why-i-wasnt-writing/.

British journalist Peter Hitchens made a compelling point when he declared, "Those who wonder what they would have done if they had lived at the time of some terrible injustice now know the answer. We do live in such a time. And we do nothing."[2] When we consider how many children have been brutally killed, and how long the killing has been allowed to continue, it is clear that we who call ourselves pro-life need to stand up stronger and speak out louder. We need to change how we present the pro-life position, ensuring that we are being clear and concise. We need to change how we communicate with people, speaking always and only with compassion.

This book follows the formidable stack of pro-life literature that has come before it—books that are important and valuable tools to the pro-life movement and neither should nor need to be replaced. This book draws on all of the knowledge that these texts present and adds countless hours of personal conversation experience. The apologetics found on these pages are not necessarily new, but they are presented in a way that has proven to be effective when used on the streets. A large team of advocates have taken these arguments to the streets, testing and re-testing them until they found the most effective way to convey the pro-life position to the public.

Not all stories end the way Sam's story did. There are other stories, stories where people were prepared with an answer when they were asked: "What do you think about abortion?" The answers they gave and the conversations that happened have resulted in the lives of children being saved. These people knew what to say because they cared enough to *learn* what to say. We may be afraid, and that is

---

2   Hitchens, Peter. "Abortion… when human life isn't just cheap, it's on special offer," *Daily* mail.com, *Peter Hitchens's blog,* May 24, 2008. https://hitchensblog.mailonsunday.co.uk/2008/05/abortion-when-h.html.

understandable. Discussing abortion with people is not easy; it is a deeply emotional topic that often dredges up feelings of anger, loss, guilt, and regret. Initiating these conversations can be intimidating, and often we are afraid of saying the wrong thing. Pro-lifers have been branded as uncompassionate people in favour of restricting the freedom of others, and because of this, many of us avoid speaking out at all.

This book is meant to change that. While recognizing that it can be difficult to engage people in discussion about abortion, the importance of doing so cannot be overstated. The conversations that we have can mean the difference between life and death; if we do not take the opportunities that we are given to speak on behalf of the pre-born, more children *will* die. The good news is that there are simple arguments which are easy to remember, and they can help us clearly articulate the pro-life position with confidence and compassion. These arguments enable us to have effective conversations that may last anywhere from thirty seconds to three hours. Having an effective conversation means more than "winning" an argument. It means more than holding our own or communicating a point. It means that real children are alive today, alive not because of a dramatic intervention by people who put their lives on the line, but because someone, somewhere took the time to have a conversation, to answer questions, to offer desperate mothers another way. The following pages are meant to equip those in the pro-life movement to answer the common questions of the abortion debate in real time, with real people.

Part One: Circumstances

Who are we talking about? The mother.
Who do we need to talk about? Her child.

"To draw an analogy: a man's suffering is similar to the behavior of a gas. If a certain quantity of gas is pumped into an empty chamber, it will fill the chamber completely and evenly, no matter how big the chamber. Thus suffering completely fills the human soul and conscious mind, no matter whether the suffering is great or little. Therefore the 'size' of human suffering is absolutely relative."

Viktor E. Frankl, *Man's Search for Meaning*

1.1 Introduction

It was a cloudy day, and while there had been signs of summer only yesterday, the air had just enough of a bite to make us wear light jackets. We set up our pro-life display outside a high school, ready to speak to students on their lunch break. This was something we did nearly every day, but when the doors of the school opened and students began pouring outside, we felt almost immediately that this time was different. There were six of us, and five minutes after the lunch bell rang, we were each surrounded by a mob of students.

"Is this about abortion?" they demanded. When I told them that it was, the students around me began to fire off questions. The air was thick with tension. Some of the girls were crying, others were angrily shaking their heads. A young man in a baggy silver jacket crouched in front of me and began to smoke a cigarette.

"What if no one wants the kid?" he demanded, flicking the ash from his cigarette off of his white sneakers. "I grew up in foster care and it stinks."

"Yeah, and what if a woman has been sexually assaulted?" a girl in a striped shirt added, her question met by a chorus of agreement.

"My mom was told she would die if she didn't have an abortion."

"There's already too much suffering in the world."

"We can't have kids, we're just kids ourselves!"

Answering each question individually was impossible, and as I tried my best to address their concerns, the questions kept coming. Each question was phrased differently, but they all had a common theme. *What about suffering?* the students were asking. *Aren't there times when abortion is really a woman's only option?* To the teenagers around me, suffering was a real thing, and abortion was a real solution.

1.2 The First Obstacle

When someone is asked the simple question, "What do you think about abortion?" the reply is often: "Well, I guess I'm pro-choice." When asked why, there are many answers one might give. One person might say, "I'm pro-choice, because no child should be unwanted." Another might ask, "What if the mother is still in school, and can't afford to raise a child?" Yet another might bring up the lack of support many pregnant mothers have, or ask about the health problems that a baby or mother may be faced with. When a discussion about abortion is initiated, often the first obstacle brought up is the difficult circumstances that can surround an unplanned pregnancy.

It isn't easy talking to people about abortion. The situations that people bring up *are* difficult, but as we focus on the humanity of the pre-born child, these circumstances may become secondary to us. In our eagerness to defend the pro-life position, it can be easy to forget that when different situations arise, they are very real, and sometimes, they are very personal. While the situation may be secondary to us, it is not secondary to the person who brought it up.

Most people can agree that abortion is not an easy choice; one does not decide to get an abortion in the same way they decide to go to the mall. Pro-choice-turned-pro-life columnist Frederica Matthewes-Green wrote the following in an article entitled "Seeking Abortion's Middle Ground": "There is a tremendous sadness and loneliness in the cry 'A woman's right to choose.' No one wants an abortion as she wants an ice-cream cone or a Porsche. She wants an abortion as an animal, caught in a trap, wants to gnaw off its own leg."[1]

Abortions of convenience certainly happen. The Guttmacher Institute, otherwise known as the research arm of Planned Parenthood[2], published a study in 2005 that noted that the most common reason cited for having an abortion was that "having a baby would dramatically change my life,"[3] which, of course, is a very safe assumption to make. That said, reasons such as poverty and age were also recorded a significant number of times. When someone brings up circumstances in which they feel abortion may be necessary, they want us to recognize that these difficult situations are the reality that many women face. They want confirmation that we understand that we are talking about real women who are struggling and needing help. It is imperative that we, as pro-lifers, understand that for many people abortion seems to be the only good alternative to an impossible situation. For many, abortion appears to be their only escape.

1.3 A Conversation Gap

The main challenge we face in conversation is a difference in focus. Those we dialogue with often focus all their attention on the fear, uncertainty, and even desperation that a woman faced with an unplanned pregnancy may be feeling. While as pro-lifers we recognize the painful reality of these circumstances, in conversations about

---

1   Frederica Matthews-Green, "Seeking Abortion's Middle Ground," frederica.com, July 28, 1996, http://frederica.com/writings/seeking-abortions-middle-ground.html.

2   Planned Parenthood is the largest abortion provider in the United States.

3   Lawrence B. Finer, et al., "Reasons U.S. Women Have Abortions: Quantitative and Qualitative Perspectives," *Guttmacher Institute*, September 2005, https://www.guttmacher.org/journals/psrh/2005/reasons-us-women-have-abortions-quantitative-and-qualitative-perspectives.

abortion we focus on the important question that Scott Klusendorf, president of Life Training Institute, emphasizes as the foundation of all pro-life apologetics: *What are the pre-born?*[4] Morally speaking, we know the question is not about circumstances. After all, if the pre-born child *is* a human being, abortion, which violently ends his or her life, is completely unethical. On the other hand, if the pre-born child is *not* a human being, then abortion is the moral equivalent of getting a tooth pulled.[5] The question we must ask is not whether circumstances are hard; rather, we must ask whether the pre-born child is a human being.

However, when considering circumstances as secondary issues, there is the danger that some pro-lifers will consider the conditions surrounding pregnancy to be not only secondary, but completely irrelevant. We may be tempted to assume that circumstances don't actually matter, but for many people the circumstances are *all* that matter, and to them, these situations are often more than enough to justify an abortion. Our goal is to convince others that pre-born children are human beings with human rights, and as such, circumstances do not justify abortion. Their goal is usually different. What they want us to understand is that the reality many women face is far from ideal. Their focus is on the mother; our focus is on her child. There is a gap in focus here, and we must close it.

1.4 Bridging the Gap

Bridging the gap between the circumstances surrounding a pregnancy, to the humanity of the pre-born child, can be done by applying three steps. The following strategies are

---

4   Scott Klusendorf, *Pro-life 101: A Step-by-Step Guide to Making Your Case Persuasively* (CA: Stand to Reason Press, 2002), 3.

5   Scott Klusendorf, "Advanced ProLife Apologetics Biola," www.caseforlife.com (2010): 5.

not only effective in focusing conversations about difficult circumstances, but they positively direct every conversation we may have:

1. Find **Common Ground**
2. Use **Analogies**
3. Ask **Questions**[6]

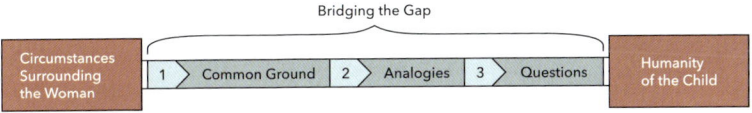

Figure 1.1 *How can we bridge this gap in focus?*
(image credit: Blaise Alleyne)

A. Common Ground

The starting place in every conversation is to find common ground. It is important that the person we are speaking with recognizes that we are interested in having a conversation, rather than feeling as if we are telling them what to do. When we realize that there is something we can agree on, we break down barriers, making it less of a narrative and more of a conversation.

Wait, you may be thinking. *What do I, as a pro-lifer in a conversation about abortion, have in common with someone advocating for "reproductive freedom"? They think that abortion is a choice we can make, a necessary evil, and I absolutely do not.* How do we find common ground with someone who believes that abortion is necessary in some situations? The answer is simple: **We can all agree that certain circumstances are**

---

6   Taught by Scott Klusendorf and Steve Wagner, executive director of Justice for All.

difficult to be faced with.[7] To be pregnant and poor would be hard. To be pregnant and young would be hard. To be pregnant and to find out your child may have health issues would be hard. Finding common ground, it turns out, is surprisingly easy. When someone makes the case for legal access to abortion by asking "what if the woman is poor?" we can begin by replying that we, too, think it would be difficult to be pregnant and poor. If someone claims to be pro-choice because teenage girls should have that option, we can find common ground by saying, "I agree with you, to be pregnant and young would be difficult."

Above all, we must be sincere. If we don't really believe that it would be difficult to be a pregnant teenager, we should step back and consider it. As the old saying goes, "Walk a mile in her shoes." Look through her eyes, and imagine what it would be like to have no support, to be scared of the future, and to feel as if the hopes and dreams you had for your life are slipping away. If we stop and think, we can see that we *do* have common ground; we can agree that these circumstances would be extremely difficult. Perhaps we can even understand how women, trapped in these circumstances, feel as if they have no other way out.

While retaining that perspective, we need to convey that we understand. We must show people that we have heard them, that we are considering everything they are saying, and that we care. Demonstrating that we are both willing to listen to them and genuinely interested in their perspective often leads to open dialogue, where both parties respectfully listen to each other's point of view.

B. Analogy

The second step in bridging the conversation gap is to use analogies, or, to tell stories. Analogies enable us to

---

7   Stephanie Gray, *Love Unleashes Life* (Toronto: Life Cycle Books, 2016), 30.

communicate our perspective in a way that will help people better understand what we are trying to say. While we may be tempted to use phrases such as "Abortion is murder!" to get our point across, these slogans are counterproductive in conversation. Rather than facilitating discussion, these types of phrases can be inflammatory and shut down a conversation before it even begins. What we want to do is paint a picture, to make the situation we are discussing more real. This idea is similar to the writing advice every first-year university English student receives: *show, don't tell.* In discussions about abortion, often a simple analogy can make all the difference.

An analogy can be used in a variety of ways. It could mean using simpler terms, or being vulnerable and sharing a personal experience. It could involve recalling a story heard on the radio that morning, or drawing connections to historical events. While there isn't a textbook of which analogies to use and when, there is one tool we can equip ourselves with that is very effective in making a concise pro-life case. This tool enables us to move the conversation from focusing on the circumstances surrounding a pregnancy to the humanity of the pre-born child. We must create a "real life" situation that people can easily identify with. This is called "trotting out the toddler," as taught by Klusendorf in *Pro-Life 101.* When trotting out the toddler we take each circumstance that has been brought up and put a toddler in the place of the pre-born child. We ask the person we are speaking with to imagine that instead of a pre-born child whose mother is very young, we have a toddler whose mother is in that same situation. This simple illustration shows that we value human beings because of the inherent dignity they possess as members of the human family (not only when they bring us joy). Most importantly, the purpose in this is to show that **circumstances, no matter how difficult they are, do not justify ending the life of an innocent human being.**

C. Question

Asking questions is the final and most important step, both to bridge the gap and to advance conversations. If we *tell* someone what we believe, they are far more likely to tune us out, ignore our arguments—no matter how logical they may be—and say, "No, that's what *you* believe. That's not what *I* think." In contrast, questions show that we are willing to *listen*, and that our goal is not to tell others what to believe, but to have an honest and open discussion. In addition, questions are a way of checking in on our conversations to make sure that we are making progress. They are crucial in that they help people realize what they already know: We don't kill human beings because of their circumstances.

After we have used an analogy to "trot out the toddler," we can ask the fundamental question: "If we may not kill a born child because of any of these circumstances, why may we kill a pre-born child in the same situation?" In some cases, this question surprises people, helping them realize that their position is not logical. They have established that they know that the way to respond to human suffering is with compassion, but often their answer will contradict this principle.

"That's different!" they might say. "The born child is a human being, but whatever is inside a pregnant woman is not!" What then, we may wonder, was achieved here? We have proven that killing is not an ethical solution to difficult life circumstances. If the person we are speaking with believes that it is wrong to kill an innocent *born* human being, but does not believe that the same is true of a *pre-born* human being, then our disagreement is not actually about the circumstances. Rather, our disagreement is about whether pre-born human beings are different from born human beings in any morally relevant way. Many abortion supporters believe that abortion is defensible because the pre-born child is not a human being, which means that the next stage of our conversation must be focused on showing that the pre-born child *is* a human being. By asking important questions, we have successfully bridged the gap from speaking about difficult circumstances to the humanity of the child in order to have that very conversation.

Testimony Spotlight

"What do you think about abortion?" I asked a woman walking by.

"I think abortion is awful; I'm pro-life," she replied.

"Great, me too!" I said, but before sending her on her way, I wanted to clarify something. "Is there any situation where you think abortion might be necessary?"

"Well, if a woman isn't going to be able to care for her children, of if the child has disabilities, I think abortion should still be an option for women."

I agreed with her that these would be difficult situations, and then asked her to imagine a born child in the same circumstances. I asked her, "Would we justify ending the life of a born child who was suffering or who had disabilities?"

When she was leaving she told me that her view had changed: "**I am definitely pro-life in every situation.** I would never allow my daughters, relatives, or friends to have an abortion. There are more options and we need to find more help for women in difficult situations."

~ Janelle Neels

Questions are vital to our conversations. In the first section, we have used questions to bring the conversation to where we need it to be. In the second section, questions such as "What do you mean by that?" or "Am I correct in understanding that you believe . . .?" or even a simple "Why?" can help clarify a point, and better enable us to see where a person is at, as well as show us what points of the pro-life position we need to focus on.[8]

1.5 In Practice

When a conversation is initially focused on difficult circumstances, bridging the gap effectively brings the focus to where we need it to be. As such, having concrete knowledge of how this system works is important. In order to show how simple it can be to use **common ground, analogies,** and **questions**, the following examples illustrate how to move the conversation from talking about the circumstances of an unplanned pregnancy to talking about the pre-born child.

A. Unwantedness

Imagine that you are in a coffee shop, and you strike up a conversation with a friendly young man. He asks what you are passionate about, and you reply that you are interested in making sure that all human beings have human rights. He looks intrigued, and asks you what your focus is.

"The rights of pre-born children," you say. "What do you think about abortion?"

His face falls ever so slightly, but he answers, "Well, I'm pro-choice. I believe that everyone has the right to be wanted and loved."

---

8   This method of questioning is clearly outlined in Peter Kreeft's *The Unaborted Socrates: A Dramatic Debate on the Issues Surrounding Abortion* (Illinois: InterVarsity Press, 1983).

"I also believe that everyone should be loved and wanted," you reply. "How does that make you pro-choice?"

He thinks for a moment. "Because if a child is unwanted, they're going to have a miserable life. It's really better off if the mother just has an abortion."

"I agree with you, to be unwanted would be incredibly painful," you concur, finding **common ground**. "What if, though, a woman becomes pregnant and decides that she's going to carry her child to term? She gives birth to her child but realizes that a child was a lot more work than she thought. She neglects to take proper care of the child, and she is passed from home to home, unwanted." You complete your **analogy** by asking: "Should we kill that child?"

A look of horror passes over the man's face. "Of course not!"

"Totally wrong, of course," you agree quickly, and follow up with the important **question**: "However, if we may not end the life of a born child because she's unwanted, why then may we end the life of a pre-born child because she's unwanted?"

He looks stumped for a moment, and then says, "You're comparing apples to oranges. A born child is a human being, independent of her mother, living and breathing. Before it is born it's just a clump of cells."

At this point in the conversation, we can transition to talking about the humanity of the pre-born child, which is what we need to focus on. It is important to know that dealing with the question of unwantedness can be a bit more complicated than the above conversation, because every conversation has its own unique challenges. The main point that we must communicate is that we do not have human rights because other people believe we have value. We have human rights because we are human beings. A homeless person still has human rights, even if no one seems to love him or want to see him on the corner of their street. Children who have bad experiences in the foster care system are still human beings with inherent dignity, even if some people consider them unwanted. Ultimately, the label "unwanted" says nothing about the people themselves, and volumes about those who label them that way. When our human rights rest on how other people value us, there are always devastating consequences.

Setting the Record Straight

Adoption

While people claim that there are many unwanted children, referencing the number of children in the foster care system, the reality is not that children—in North America specifically—are unwanted, but rather that there are major flaws in both the adoption and foster care systems. While numerous couples eagerly wait to adopt, the adoption process is long, expensive, and often disappointing. Infants are often turned over to foster care not because there is no one willing to adopt them, but because their biological parent or parents are unable to care for them and yet are unwilling to terminate parental rights. This has resulted in many children growing up in foster care, unable to be adopted, with every passing year making it increasingly difficult for them to find a permanent home. Essentially, there are no unwanted children: there are adoptive parents longing to add children—particularly infants—to their families. This carries over to children with special needs as well, as there are many couples who specifically request a child who may have developmental challenges.

B. Poverty

Now picture yourself at a university, tabling with the campus pro-life club. As you walk around handing out invitations for the next event, a fellow student walks up to you.

"Why are you doing this?" she demands angrily. "Don't you understand that abortion is necessary?"

"Hi there," you answer politely, sensing that if you're not careful the situation may escalate. "Why do you believe that abortion is necessary?"

"Do you know how many people live in poverty? Is that what you want? Do you want more kids to go hungry? If a woman is pregnant and she knows she can't support a baby, she should totally have an abortion."

"I agree with you, that to be pregnant and poor would be really, really hard," you reply softly, finding **common ground.** You follow up with an **analogy**: "There are so many poor people in the world. Should we just go into low-income areas of town and kill the people who are suffering?"

"Don't be ridiculous!"

"Why not?"

"You can't kill people because they're poor! We ought to be setting up programs to help these people, not just killing them."

"I totally agree with you, we should eliminate problems rather than eliminate people," you say, and then ask the **question**: "If we may not kill born people because they're poor, why then may we kill pre-born children because they will be born into poverty?"

The student looks annoyed. "That is totally different!"

"How so?"

"An embryo is not the same as a human being. It's not even alive yet!"

Again, you've managed to bridge the conversational gap, proving that killing isn't an ethical solution to the difficult circumstance of poverty. As Stephanie Gray points out, our duty is to alleviate suffering rather than eliminate sufferers.[9]

C. No Support

This time, you are on a city bus that is stuck in traffic. The young man sitting next to you adjusts his baseball cap, takes off his earphones, and strikes up a conversation with you. During your discussion, you have a perfect opportunity to ask:

"What do you think about abortion?"

"Dude, I don't know." He looks as if he wishes he was in the aisle seat so he could escape. "I guess I'm pro-choice. You know, if someone's going to get kicked out of the house if they keep the baby, then they should have an abortion. I mean, who wants to be all alone in that kind of situation?"

"I agree with you, to be pregnant and have no support would be really hard," you say (**common ground**). "Now, I want you to imagine that a young woman carries through with a pregnancy and gives birth, but after her baby is a few months old, her parents get sick of the situation and kick her and the baby out of the house. She's all alone. Should she be allowed to kill her baby?" (**analogy**)

"That's totally sick, of course not! She can, like, bring her baby somewhere or something."

---

9   Stephanie Gray, *Love Unleashes Life* (Toronto: Life Cycle Books, 2016), 92.

"Definitely, you and I can agree that there are better options and better choices that she could make. So let's go back for a second. If she's not allowed to kill her born child because she has no support, why then may she kill her pre-born child because she has no support?" (**question**)

He thinks for a moment. "I see what you're saying, man, but don't you think that's a bit different?"

"How is it different?"

"Well, I mean, the baby is, like, a baby. When it isn't born yet it's not really anything."

"So, am I right in thinking that you believe that a baby is a human being but an embryo or a fetus is not?"

"Yeah, that's what I mean!"

Again, you have managed to establish that killing is not an ethical solution to difficult life circumstances and focused the conversation on the status of the pre-born child. The important thing to notice here is that you managed to stay on track, concentrating on bringing the conversation to where it needs to be. There are so many other issues that you could bring up. You could talk about how there are pregnancy care centres in every city, ready and waiting to offer women the support that they need. You could talk about how we should educate parents on how to respond when their daughter or son is facing an unplanned pregnancy, or how to talk with their children about sexuality. While all these points are very important, they are not what we need to focus on when we are in a discussion about abortion. In such a conversation, our focus must be on the humanity of the pre-born child, and the brutal nature of abortion. You may have a chance to talk about these issues later in the conversation, but it is vital that we remain focused on the pre-born child. We must always remember that we only have a limited amount of time with the person we are speaking with, and we want to be certain that we have given a concise, clear, and compelling case for the rights of pre-born children.

D. Age/Education

Airplanes are both wonderful and scary. You often have the opportunity to meet very interesting people, but you could also end up sitting beside someone you would rather not spend five hours with. Imagine that in this case, though, the lady beside you is in a far more uncomfortable position than you are, because you've just asked her what she thinks about abortion.

"Well, it's a very important right for women," she asserts confidently. "After all, when you're young and in the middle of your education, the last thing you need is a child."

"I agree with you that it would be difficult to be a young student and have a child," you say (**common ground**). "Imagine this: a young student gets pregnant, but she thinks that she can handle it. She has her baby, but soon realizes that piles of homework and late-night feedings are difficult to keep up with. She's at the end of her rope; should she be allowed to kill her baby?" (**analogy**)

"Don't be ridiculous!" she scoffs. "I see what you're trying to do here, but it's not going to work with me. You can't compare a baby with a pregnancy!"

"I do want to ask one thing: if we may not kill a born child because of difficult circumstances, why should we be allowed to kill pre-born children?" (**question**).

"I told you! Because they're not children at all. They're not even humans yet!"

Of course, the conversation doesn't end here. You still have three hours of the flight left to go, which gives you plenty of time to explain to your seat mate how the pre-born *are*, in fact, human beings, something we will learn how to do in Part Two. At this point, though, it is enough to point out that once again we have bridged the conversational gap, going from discussing a difficult situation, to what will truly settle this moral dilemma: the humanity of pre-born children.

1.6 Conclusion

Conversations do not always work out exactly as planned. Each conversation will be unique, and each person we speak with will have slightly different responses to our questions. This emphasizes the importance of experience: the more people we engage, the more prepared we will be to communicate the pro-life position well. From countless hours of successful pro-life outreach, we are convinced that by finding common ground, using analogies, and asking questions we can lead the conversation to the focus it needs: the humanity of the pre-born child. There will be detours, and certainly some dips and corners in our conversations, but as long as we seek to understand the person in front of us, we can expect to have profitable encounters.

What next? you may ask. In short: find more common ground, tell more stories, and ask more questions.

Key Takeaways

- The 1st conversational obstacle: Difficult circumstances—*Does the suffering that can accompany an unplanned pregnancy ever justify having an abortion?*

- A pro-lifer's focus: Who the pre-born are and what abortion does to them. An abortion supporter's focus: How a woman in a crisis pregnancy may be feeling. *This gap in focus needs to be bridged.*

- Bridging the gap:

    - *Common Ground*: Find something that you and the person you are speaking with can agree on.

    - *Analogy*: Use stories to paint a picture and illustrate your point.

    - *Questions*: Let the person you are speaking with explain their position. Draw their position out with questions that show genuine interest in their perspective and help them think through their own arguments.

1.7 Diving Deeper

1. Imagine: You are living in poverty and have no support from loved ones. You have just discovered you are pregnant. How are you feeling?

2. When a woman finds herself pregnant in a difficult

situation how do you think she will respond to the following statements:

A. Abortion is murder! How could you even consider doing that to your baby?

B. How did you get yourself into this position in the first place?

C. How are you feeling?

D. Is there any way I can help?

1.8 Suggested Activities

1. With a partner, choose one of the following difficult circumstances and use common ground, analogies, and questions to bring the conversation from the point of talking about circumstances to talking about the humanity of the pre-born child.

A. A single mother with two children is living in poverty. She does not have a job and has no support from her family.

B. A teenage girl in high school with straight A's and a good chance of winning a complete scholarship to university.

C. A woman in an abusive relationship with her partner, who threatens to throw her out if she doesn't have an abortion.

D. A forty-year-old career woman who is just about to receive the promotion she's been working towards for a decade.

2. With a partner, go through different difficult

circumstances and practice trotting out the toddler, where you remove the pre-born child from the circumstance and replace him or her with a born child in the same situation.

3. Start a discussion with a parent, sibling, or friend. Practice using common ground, analogies, and questions to make your point.

1.9 Additional Resources

• *Love Unleashes Life — Stephanie Gray*

- This apologetics book introduced many of the strategies discussed in this resource. It offers more examples as well as engaging stories to help solidify important concepts.

• *Tactics: A Game Plan for Discussing Your Christian Convictions — Gregory Koukl*

- While this book is not specifically about abortion, it teaches many effective conversational strategies and gives helpful tips on how to maintain control of a discussion and steer it in the direction you want it to go.

• *The Unaborted Socrates: A Dramatic Debate on the Issues Surrounding Abortion — Peter Kreeft*

- This book gives fantastic examples of how to use questioning to steer a conversation and facilitate discussion. It delves deeper into many of the issues surrounding abortion that will be discussed in later parts of this resource.

-

Part Two: Human Rights

A whole, distinct, living human being comes into existence at the moment of fertilization; abortion violates the most fundamental right of this human being.

*"To deny people their human rights
is to challenge their very humanity."*
Nelson Mandela

2.1 Introduction

"What do you think about abortion?" I asked a young man. His brown curls were slightly scraggly, as if the hood of his red sweatshirt had been pulled off moments before. He shrugged.

"I'm not really sure," he said, scuffing his black sneaker against the sidewalk. "I'm a guy, so it's never really been something I thought I needed to worry about."

"Fair enough," I replied. "Do you believe in human rights?"

He thought for a moment. "Yeah, I do."

"Great, me too! You had me worried there for a second," I joked. "By the way, my name is Justina."

He took my outstretched hand and shook it firmly. "Mine's Isaiah."

"So, Isaiah, you said that you believe in human rights. Who do you think should get human rights?"

He looked confused for a second, as if I had asked a stupid question. "Ummm. Every living human being?"

"Makes sense to me," I agreed. "And if two human beings reproduce, what will their offspring be?"

"Obviously human." Isaiah shifted awkwardly, as if he had someplace better to be than a sidewalk in front of his school with a girl asking him too many questions.

"Right!" I said, realizing I had to wrap this conversation up. "Since the pre-born child must be a human being, and we believe in human rights for everyone, isn't abortion a human rights violation?"

Isaiah looked surprised. "Woah," he said. "I never thought of it that way. Abortion *must* be wrong."

2.2 The Fundamental Question

The effective tactic of bridging the gap leads us to the pivotal question of the abortion debate: **What are the pre-born?** As Greg Koukl from Stand to Reason asserts, "If the [pre-]born is not a human being, no justification for abortion is necessary. However, if the [pre-]born is a human being, no justification for abortion is adequate."[1] It is essential for us to understand that the principle difference between the pro-choice and pro-life views are not their feelings towards abortion, but rather their understanding of the nature of the pre-born. This knowledge indicates two important points: we must be informed on basic biology, and we must be able to communicate this knowledge to others in a clear manner.

Conversations about abortion often come to a stand-still once we get to the point where we must agree on the nature of the pre-born. It is here that we employ the **human rights argument**,[2] which consists of four of the most important questions we will ever ask:

1. *Do you believe in human rights?*

2. *Who should have human rights?*

3. *If two human beings reproduce, what will their offspring be?*

4. *If something is growing, isn't it alive?*

---

1   Greg Koukl, "Only One Question,"*Stand to Reason,* February 28, 2013, https://www.str.org/articles/only-one-question#.WVO_SzOZO8o.

2   The human rights argument was developed by the staff of the Canadian Centre for Bio-Ethical Reform while doing pro-life outreach.

2.3 Human Rights

The first question, **Do you believe in human rights?**, emphasizes essential **common ground.** The answer to this question is nearly always a reflex one: "Of course I do!" Most people understand that the recognition of fundamental human rights is the foundation of any civil society. Human rights protect us from one another. A brief look into the past tells us this protection is absolutely necessary, which will be discussed more extensively in Part 3. Further, asking this simple question will reveal immediately if a conversation is worth having. If someone does not believe in human rights, there is very little that can be said, other than attempting to explain how dangerous such a worldview can be. The few who claim they do not believe in human rights may understand the implications of what they say and be willing to accept them—in theory. It is important not to give up on these conversations too early, as in many cases testing their beliefs using **analogies** often makes them reconsider their position (discussed in more depth in Part 4). However, the majority of people firmly assert their belief in human rights, and this secures immediate common ground, providing an anchor that we can consistently return to in our advocacy for the pre-born.

This leads us to the second question, which is intricately entwined with the first: **Who should have human rights?** This question seems redundant, as the phrase *human rights* overtly states to whom the rights belong. Even so, it is important to recognize that oversimplification can be an effective type of clarification. Further, what appears obvious to us—human rights belong to human beings—may not be as obvious to others. In fact, we may define *human beings* differently. In this case, many people do not believe pre-born children are human beings, and therefore do not believe that the pre-born are entitled to human rights. What this informs us is that when we are told: *"Human beings* should have human rights," or *"Everyone* should have human rights," people will not naturally translate this belief over to pre-born children.

As an illustration, the UN Women Executive Director powerfully stated in a message published on Human Rights Day, "Our hopes for a more just, safe and peaceful world can only be achieved when there is universal respect for the inherent dignity and equal rights of **all members of the human family**" (emphasis added).[3] As pro-lifers, we would firmly agree with this statement, as pre-born children are scientifically proven to be part of the human family. This statement should ensure human rights for pre-born children as well. However, in complete contradiction to this statement, UN Women published a report in 2014 entitled "Gender Equality and Sustainable Development," emphasizing control over "reproductive health"—a common way to refer to abortion without directly mentioning it—as a woman's right. The report stated, "The human rights of women include their right to have control over and decide freely and responsibly on matters related to their sexuality, including sexual and **reproductive health** . . ."(emphasis added).[4] Clearly, they did not consider pre-born children as part of the human family, with the same inherent dignity as the rest of us.

This again emphasizes the importance of the question: "What are the pre-born?" If the pre-born are human beings,

3   Phumzile Mlambo-Ngcuka, "Message of UN Women Executive Director Phumzile Mlambo-Ngcuka on Human Rights Day," *UN Women,* December 9, 2013, http://www.unwomen.org/en/news/stories/2013/12/ed-message-on-international-human-rights-day.

4   The Research and Data section of UN Women. "World Survey on the role of Women in Development 2014: Gender Equality and Sustainable Development," *UN Women* (2014): 78. http://www.unwomen.org/~/media/headquarters/attachments/sections/library/publications/2014/unwomen_surveyreport_advance_16oct.pdf.

then it logically follows that they, too, are entitled to human rights. In order to answer that question, we need to turn to the third question of the human rights argument.

Testimony Spotlight

"Did you know that abortion is legal through all nine months of pregnancy in Canada?" I asked a teenage girl.

"No!" she said, shocked. "I didn't know that. I don't agree with abortion when the baby is older. But in the first couple weeks, I don't really see the problem with it."

"Do you believe in human rights?"

"Of course!"

"And who should get human rights?"

"Humans."

"If two human beings reproduce, what species are their offspring?"

She hesitated. "Human, I guess."

"Then doesn't it follow that abortion is a human rights violation?" I finished.

Her eyes widened. "Yes, yes it does!" she said, nodding. "It's not okay to kill a child, I get that now."

~ Cana Méndez Campos

2.4 What are its parents?

When we ask the third question of the human rights argument—If two human beings reproduce, what will their offspring be?—we exercise the simplest way to determine the species to which an organism belongs. Every living organism receives their DNA from parent or parents. Their DNA ensures that their species-membership is encoded into every cell of their body. In the case of human beings, biology informs us that with the union of a sperm cell and an oocyte (egg), a whole, distinct, living human being comes

Clarifying Terms

Human Parts vs. Human Wholes

At times it is necessary to clarify the difference between human parts and human wholes. Because human life begins with a single-celled embryo, people sometimes struggle with the idea that this particular cell is different than any other kind of cell. We are often confronted with questions such as: "I just brushed off hundreds of skin cells. Am I a murderer?" or with the popular slogan: "Is masturbation murder?" The answer to these questions is simple: of course not! Skin cells and sperm cells are both **human parts**. They will never grow and develop into mature human beings because they are not **human wholes**. Embryos, on the other hand, will grow and develop into mature human beings, if nothing unnatural interrupts that development. He or she is a young human being, not yet mature, whereas skin cells and sperm cells are not.

into existence, namely, an embryo. The embryo is distinct (unless, of course, he or she is an identical twin); she has received half of her DNA from her father and half from her mother, resulting in a unique combination of genes that has never existed before and will never exist again.

Science proves that the embryo is human, as her parents are human; the sperm and egg cells that came together to create the embryo were human parts designed to create a human whole. The science is simple, so simple, in fact, that it is hardly necessary to explain; living things reproduce after their own kind. We know that human beings must reproduce human beings in the same way that dogs reproduce dogs, ducks reproduce ducks, and frogs reproduce frogs. When someone tells us that she is expecting, do we ever think to ask her, "Expecting what?" Further, when the same person calls us to share that her child has arrived, do we ever exclaim in relief that we are glad she had a human baby, because she could have had a puppy, kitten, or duckling? These examples are simplifications, illustrating a straight-forward concept. However, what we view as common sense is, sadly, no longer common knowledge.

A. It's just a fetus!

The reason reproductive biology is no longer understood is because the pro-choice movement has successfully clouded basic facts, vaguely referring to "clumps of cells," "products of conception," or "the pregnancy." Even the correct scientific terms for pre-born children have been badly misused. This becomes evident when we are met with confusion while trying to explain that an embryo or a fetus must be a human being because her parents are human. "How can you think that is a human being," a student may ask, "when you just called it an embryo?" "Exactly!" another student might exclaim. "A fetus isn't a human being, it's a *fetus*!" The terms "embryo" and "fetus" have in some ways

Testimony Spotlight

"What are you doing here?" A man angrily asked me, after storming up to our pro-life display.

"Hello, sir," I answered politely. "**Do you believe in human rights?**"

"Yeah, I do, but it's a woman's choice!" He continued, trying to get his thoughts in order: "If they want to kill . . . if they want to have an abortion . . . if it was murder, the police would charge them with murder!"

"**Who gets human rights?**" I asked him.

"Well, we all do," he replied.

"**If two human beings reproduce, what species are their offspring?**"

He rolled his eyes. "I don't know, I don't have kids."

"From biology class, **we know that humans reproduce humans**," I explained, and when he nodded in agreement I continued, "If we have a human being, and human rights are supposed to be for everyone, **what about the pre-born child's human rights?**" As he continued nodding, I explained that we educate people on who the pre-born are and what abortion does to them because the children killed by abortion deserve human rights as well.

"You're right," he said. "You're right. Sorry for snapping at you."

~ Blaise Alleyne

become dehumanizing; they have been used to refer to the pre-born as a sort of sub-class of human, or even as another species entirely. As a result, many pro-lifers have rejected these terms as tools of the pro-choice movement.

However, while we need to address the confusion regarding wording, we do not need to reject these terms outright. Rather, we should clarify these terms with a question: "What kind of fetus?"[5] This query is often met with a blank look, because many people do not realize that human beings are not the only creatures that have fetuses. In fact, the offspring of all *viviparous organisms*—organisms that bring forth live young that have developed within their bodies—develop through embryonic and fetal stages. This means that the terms embryo and fetus are not species-specific. Dogs, blue whales, and snow leopards all have fetuses. These terms do not tell us *what something* is, they merely tell us *how old someone* is. The labels embryo and fetus are merely age-classifications in the same way that infant, toddler, teenager, and adult are. In fact, the word *fetus* is derived from Latin, meaning young one, or offspring.

In discussing age-classifications, it is important to note that human beings exist on a continuum. We do not change in essence when we graduate from infancy to toddlerhood, or from toddlerhood to adolescence. While entrance into adulthood finds us endowed with new civil rights, our fundamental human rights never change. The pro-life position is actually very simple: **human rights belong to human beings, and those rights begin when the human being begins.** We can answer the question of what the pre-born child is when we answer the question: "Who are her parents?" The next question we must answer is, "When does human life begin?"

---

5   This question is posed by Stephanie Gray in *Love Unleashes Life* (Toronto: Life Cycle Books, 2016), 39.

2.5 When does life begin?

As people wrestle with the idea that the pre-born child is indeed a human being, they may exclaim in frustration, "But it's not even alive!" Once again, rather than answering a claim with an explanation, we should follow it with a clarifying question. When someone makes this assertion we use the fourth question of the human rights argument: **If something is growing, isn't it alive?** We know that an embryo is growing, for there is evidence of the rapid division of cells from one to two, two to four, four to eight, and so on. If the embryo was not alive, abortion would not be necessary. What the pro-choice movement calls "the termination of a pregnancy" is ending the life of a living human being.

Many will contest that we do not know *exactly* when human life begins, so we do not need to be concerned about abortion. The answer to this contention is two-fold. First of all, if we are unsure of when human life begins, we ought to err on the side of caution. For example, if a hunter shoots wildly into the bush without being certain that it is an animal he is shooting at rather than his hunting partner, he is culpable if he—albeit unintentionally—shoots his friend. If what resides in the womb of an expectant mother *could* be a human being, and we believe in human rights, then caution in dealing with the pre-born is critical.

Secondly, this claim is completely false. There is a scientific consensus on when life begins. The embryology textbook The Developing Human: Clinically Oriented Embryology, 10th edition states the following: "Human development begins at fertilization when a sperm fuses with an oocyte to form a single cell, the zygote. [This] marks the beginning of each of us as an unique individual."[6] The basic

---

6   Moore, Persaud, Torchia, *The Developing Human: Clinically Oriented Embryology, 10th edition.* Philadelphia, PA: Elsevier, 2016. p. 11.

psychology introductory textbook Psychology: Themes and Variations, 3rd edition asserts that:

> "Development begins with conception. Conception occurs when fertilization creates a zygote, a one-celled organism formed by the union of a sperm and an egg. All other cells in your body develop from this single cell."[7]

The Developmental Biology textbook 11th edition labels its seventh chapter, "Fertilization: Beginning of a New Organism."[8] The idea that life begins at fertilization is something we all ascribe to, simply by stating that the duration of a healthy pregnancy is nine months. This is common knowledge, and it demonstrates an understanding that something very significant happened nine months prior to birth.

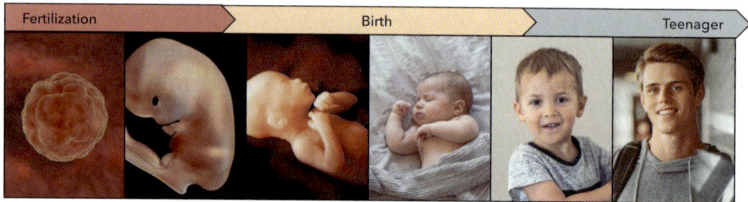

Figure 2.1 *The Continuum of Human Life*

A. Before, at, or after?

The knowledge that a significant event occurred nine months before birth is nearly universal, which means that our task is not so much to convey this understanding to the

---

7   Doug McCann & Wayne Weiten, *Psychology: Themes and Variations, 3rd Canadian edition.* Toronto, ON, 2013. p. 491.

8   Scott F. Gilbert & Michael J.F. Barresi, *Developmental Biology, 11th edition.* Massachusetts, U.S.A, 2016. p. 217.

Clarifying Terms

Fertilization vs. Conception

We often use the words conception and fertilization interchangeably. However, the word conception has changed slightly in meaning. To some, conception refers to the moment when implantation has occurred—the point at which the embryo has safely travelled down the fallopian tube and burrowed into the uterine wall, approximately nine days after fertilization has taken place. Terms are important here, because it is crucial that we are not misunderstood. Many believe that if an embryo is unable to implant in the uterus, a pregnancy never occurred. However, since life begins at fertilization, what happens in these cases is a very early miscarriage, the death of a tiny human being. While we are often not even aware of these tiny human beings, that does not negate the fact that they existed. Because no one confuses fertilization with implantation in the same way they confuse the terms conception and implantation, it is best that fertilization is the term we rely on in conversation.

person we are speaking with as to draw it out of them. We can do this by asking if they agree that life could begin at one of three points: before fertilization, at fertilization, or after fertilization.[9] After we have established that these are the three points that need to be discussed, we can begin with the first option: before fertilization. Before fertilization there

---

9   This idea was developed by Stephanie Gray and has been presented in many of her pro-life apologetics presentations.

is a sperm cell and an egg. A question that we can ask to make our case is this: "Will a sperm cell, left alone in a man's body, ever grow and develop into a mature human being?" When we have received an answer that acknowledges that this is impossible, we can follow up with a second question: "Will an egg, left alone in a woman's body, ever grow and develop into a mature human being?" Since the answer to both of these questions is undoubtedly no, we conclude that life does not begin before fertilization.

After we have agreed that life cannot begin before fertilization, we can jump to the third option: **some point after fertilization.** Again, instead of offering information, we further the conversation by asking questions. Often, the conversation will look something like this:

"Now that we have agreed that life cannot begin before fertilization, let's take the third option. Many people believe that life begins at some point after fertilization. However, would you agree that when we see a toddler walk through a door with her mom, we don't assume that the toddler came into existence at that moment, just because we've never seen her before?"

"Of course!"

"So it's fair to say we know that the toddler grew and developed from a younger version of herself, which was an infant. Infants come into existence when the stork drops them off at our doorstep, right?"

"Stop being ridiculous."

"I am being ridiculous, aren't I? That idea is crazy to us because we know that infants grew and developed from younger versions of themselves, namely fetuses. And do women wake up in the middle of the night with a swollen abdomen and a fetus squirming and kicking inside of them as their introduction to pregnancy?"

"No, the fetus grew and developed from an embryo."

"Right! And where did the embryo come from?"

"Well, I don't know . . . Fertilization?"

"Exactly. **At the moment of fertilization a whole, distinct, living human being comes into existence.** Neither of us can say that we were once a sperm or that we were once an egg, but we both can say that we were once infants, fetuses, and embryos. All human beings can trace their lives back to the moment of fertilization."

Setting the Record Straight

Cloning

When we point out that a single cell, **left on its own**, can never grow and develop into a mature human being, the phrase left on its own is very important. Pro-choice advocates at times like to reference cloning to prove that a skin cell *could* one day grow and develop into a mature human being. However, cloning is a complicated, extensive process. In fact, reproductive cloning—which has been used to clone animals such as Dolly the sheep—uses two cells rather than just one, and **requires stimulation from outside sources** in order to initiate cell division. Essentially, left on their own, a sperm cell, oocyte, or skin cell will never grow and develop into a mature human being, whereas an embryo will, evidencing the fundamental difference between these types of cells.

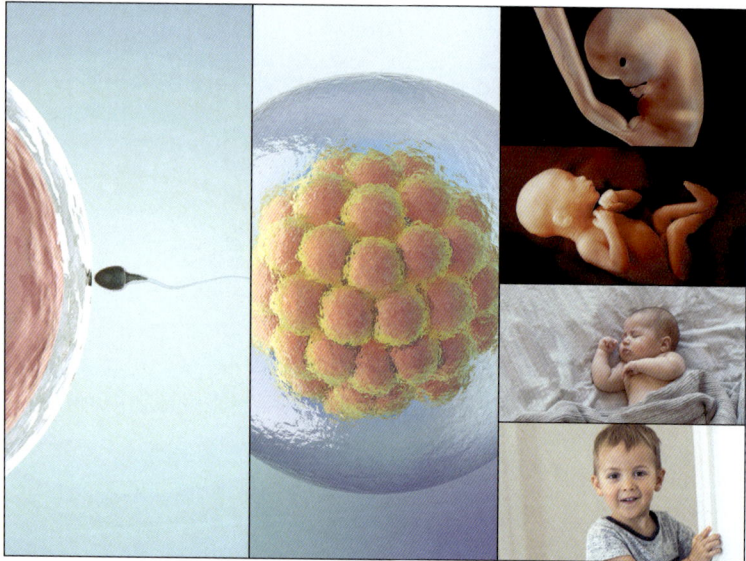

Figure 2.2 *Before, at, or after?*

Talking through the points at which people believe life begins is often helpful. However, many people still struggle with the idea that an embryo, a single cell no bigger than the period at the end of this sentence, is a human being with human rights. The early embryo seems insignificant. He or she is not recognizably human, and at this point in development, no one is even aware of his or her existence. It is important to remember that our emotional connection to people is not what gives them their value. In fact, our entire doctrine of human rights is based on the concept that human beings are *inherently* valuable. In order to illustrate the importance of recognizing the existence of a human being from the moment of fertilization, we can use the following analogy.

B. The Polaroid Analogy

The Polaroid Analogy was created by law professor

Setting the Record Straight

Embryonic Stem Cell Research

Embryonic stem cells are coveted for research due to their ability to differentiate themselves. A stem cell may become any type of cell in the body, and potentially stimulate the growth of a heart or lung. Researchers believe that in the future they may be able to grow healthy organs by stimulating embryonic stem cells, in order to reduce the need for organ donation. While we can understand the desperate desire people have to help their loved ones who need organs, **the ends never justify the means**. We may not kill a human being in order to save another human being. Because embryos are tiny human beings, creating them in order to harvest their cells for research is completely immoral and a blatant human rights violation. Further, researchers have had some success using adult stem cells. This is a possible alternative solution to supply the need for stem cells, as using embryonic stem cells ends the life of the embryo, whereas using adult stem cells does not end the life of the adult.

Richard Stith,[10] and is useful in clarifying the question of when life begins. Polaroid cameras are an older technology, but the novelty of almost-instant pictures has brought them back. Most people know what a polaroid is and how it works, but offering a quick explanation can help clarify why we are talking about these cameras in the first place. The older Polaroids looked

---

10   Richard Stith, "Arguing with Pro-Choicers," *First things,* November 2006, http://www.firstthings.com/web-exclusives/2006/11/stith-arguing-with-pro-choicer.

almost like small printers, and a blank card was inserted in the top. After the picture was taken, the white card would slide out the bottom, covered in black smudges. After a few moments, the captured image would begin to appear.

Now imagine that you have always wanted to go to England. Big Ben and Buckingham Palace have captured your imagination, and you can't wait to be surrounded by posh-sounding accents. But the real reason you want to go, the only reason that you feel it is worth it to spend the money on a plane ticket, is that you want to meet the Queen. You spend your last dollar on tickets, and realize too late that you don't have enough money to buy a camera. Thankfully, your grandmother saves the day and lends you her trusty Polaroid.

You head off to England and find out exactly where to find the royal family. You decide to stay up all night, so you can be at the very front of the barricades. It's London, so it is cold and wet, but you bear it bravely and even manage to make a new British friend. Finally, morning comes, and as the sun rises higher, at last you see carriages in the distance. Carriages with earls, carriages with dukes, and then, there she is! But it doesn't look like she is going to stop.

You wave your Canadian flag weakly, desperately disappointed. But then the Queen waves her white-gloved hand at the guard with the fluffy hat driving her carriage. He stops the horses and jumps down. "You there!" He calls out. "Her majesty doesn't have much time, but you're cold, wet, and Canadian, and so in the interest of diplomacy she will shake your hand." Trembling with excitement, you hand your Polaroid to your new friend and say, "Remember, all you need to do is click the button!" You race over to the carriage and reach out your hand. Now, you don't remember what the Queen said or even what you said, but you know that the moment your hand touched the Queen's you glanced over your shoulder and saw your friend click the shutter on your grandma's camera.

Relief floods through you as you realize that your whole trip was worth it. You run back to your friend, just in time to see her pull the card from the bottom of the camera, rip it into shreds, and throw it into a large puddle. "Oh, darling," she says apologetically. "I didn't get your picture!" Stuttering with disbelief, you manage to squeak, "But I saw you click the button!" "Yes, darling," she says, "but black smudgy stuff was all that came out." "No," you exclaim. "No! It wasn't just black smudgy stuff. Everything

From Left Field

Acorns vs. Oak Trees

Another argument against the idea that embryos and fetuses are human beings is as follows: "If we don't say that an *acorn* is an *oak tree*, why would we say that an *embryo* is a *human being*? Killing an embryo is not the same as killing a child or an adult!" First, it is important to realize that an acorn is actually a very young tree — to say that "an acorn is not an oak tree" is like saying "an embryo is not an adult." That is true, but does not prove what the person using the argument intends to prove. An acorn is a young member of the oak species, just as an embryo is a young member of the human species. However, what they may *mean* to say is that "a seed is not a tree." In this case, it is helpful to bring the conversation away from plant biology and back to mammals by asking a simple question: What is a *human* seed? To say a seed is not a tree is like saying a sperm cell is not a human being. Both of these statements are valid, however after the point of fertilization, we are no longer dealing with a human seed, but a human being (refer to section 2.5).

(The "seed is not a tree" argument was developed by Blaise Alleyne).

about the image of me shaking the Queen's hand was captured in an instant: all it needed was time to develop."

In the same way, everything about each one of us was captured in an instant: all we needed was time to develop. This Polaroid story illustrates the fact that human beings develop, they are not constructed. Pre-born children are not like cars on assembly lines. We all may have different opinions on precisely when a car becomes a car. Some may say that a car must have four wheels, a frame, and a steering wheel. Others might claim that a car becomes a car once it has a windshield. Few, if any, would claim that a car is a car from the very first screw. A car is a constructed thing.[11] An embryo, on the other hand, develops itself. Everything that is needed for development is captured in the moment of fertilization; all she needs after that point is time.

C. *Twinning*

When we assert that our lives began the instant fertilization took place, sometimes people bring up identical (monozygotic) twinning—where a single embryo splits into two—as proof that this is not the case. Twinning can occur from day two after fertilization until day ten, after which twinning is extremely rare and may result in conjoined twins. Because of the potential for an embryo to split, some say that life does not begin until after twinning can no longer occur. While this may seem as if it is a difficult question, the answer is quite simple. When a flatworm is cut in half, regeneration of body parts often occurs, resulting in two separate worms. Would we say that because a flatworm may be split, it is not a flatworm until this has taken place?[12] We know, rather, that there always was a flatworm, and

---

11   Richard Stith, "Does Making Babies Make Sense? Why so Many People Find it Difficult to See Humanity in a Developing Foetus," Mercatornet, September 2, 2008.

12   Patrick Lee, Abortion and Unborn Human Life (Washington, D.C. Catholic University Press in America, 1996) p. 93.

now there are two. In the same way, at fertilization there is a single embryo, and by some unexplainable miracle this single embryo at times will split into two embryos. This leaves the mother pregnant, not with one, but two children.

Setting the Record Straight

Protecting a species

When we talk about protecting human beings from the moment they come into existence, it can be helpful to compare how we protect humans to how we protect other species. For example, in conversation we may ask: "If we were to protect bald eagles, how would we go about doing that? Would we protect only the adult eagles? Or only the eagles who have learned how to fly?" "No," most people would reply. "We would protect all eagles." "Even the eagle eggs?" you may ask. "Of course! The eagle eggs have baby eagles in them. If we are going to protect a species, it is crucial to protect their young." If we look outside of our own species, protecting a certain group always includes the youngest members of the group as well as the older ones. Doing otherwise simply does not make sense.

D. Composition and Behaviour

If we make the claim that life begins at the point of fertilization, we must be able to back this claim up with science. In her paper "When Does Human Life Begin?" Dr. Maureen Condic explains that in order to establish what type of cell we are dealing with, scientists look at its composition and behaviour. The **single-celled embryo, also called a zygote**, needs to be examined to see whether it can be called a unique individual. When mentioning the zygote, people often refer to the "fertilized egg." In reality, there is no such thing. Condic explains that at the instant of sperm-egg fusion the sperm and egg cells no longer exist, and a cell distinct from both parent cells is created. After studying the cell composition and behaviour of the zygote versus the sperm and egg cells, Condic wrote the following:

> Based on [the] factual description of the events following sperm-egg binding, we can confidently conclude that a new cell, the zygote, comes into existence at the 'moment' of sperm-egg fusion, an event that occurs in less than a second. At the point of fusion, sperm and egg are physically united— i.e., they cease to exist as gametes, and they form a new entity that is materially distinct from either sperm or egg. The behavior of this new cell also differs radically from that of either sperm or egg: the developmental pathway entered into by the zygote is distinct from both gametes. Thus, sperm-egg fusion is indeed a scientifically well defined 'instant' in which the zygote . . . is formed.[13]

Simply put, the zygote (embryo) is distinct from both the sperm cell and egg in genetic and molecular composition, due to the merging of cells in the instant of fertilization. The zygote's behaviour is different from its parent cells. The goal of the sperm cell is to find an egg and penetrate it, while the goal of the egg cell is to permit penetration. Once penetration occurs, the zygote creates a protective shield around itself to prevent any other sperm cells from penetrating it, showing

---

13   Condic, Maureen. "When Does Human Life Begin?" *The Westchester Institute For Ethics & the Human Person, White Paper Volume 1, Number 1* (October 2008). pg. 5.

different behaviour from its parent cells from the moment of fertilization. If we are able to explain the importance of cell composition and behaviour, we are able to prove that science has indeed established that human life begins in an instant.

From Left Field

Why don't we celebrate conception days?

Another argument that pro-choice advocates use to prove that life begins at birth, is the fact that we celebrate birthdays. If life truly begins at conception, the reasoning goes, why don't we celebrate conception day? Why do we say that we are twenty years old on our birthday, when in reality we are twenty years and nine months? First of all, the celebration of birthdays is a cultural tradition that began long before there was an advanced knowledge of embryology. Further, even now it is often difficult to determine on what day, specifically, that conception occurred. Birthdays do not assume the day on which our lives began; rather, the word clearly states that it is the day on which we were born. It is common knowledge that we existed as fetuses and embryos before we were born.

E. Viability vs. Vitality

While scientific evidence proves that life begins at fertilization, some abortion supporters may struggle with accepting this. "Wait," they might say, "embryos and fetuses are not alive because they are not *viable*. They are entirely dependent on their mother's body for survival, so they cannot be an independent human being." The concept of "my body, my choice" is spoken about in detail in Part 4. The point we need to emphasize here is that there is a fundamental difference between *vitality* and *viability*, that is, being alive versus being able to survive. When a human being is outside of their natural environment, they will be unable to survive. Human beings can only survive in environments that have certain conditions. Therefore, a diver must wear a wetsuit and carry an oxygen tank and an astronaut cannot survive without a space suit. Although the diver and the astronaut would not be viable without their specialized environments, no one would deny that they are, in fact, alive. In the same way, while an embryo or fetus cannot survive outside of the womb—his or her natural environment—that does not mean that they are not alive.

Further, while medical viability is considered to be around 24 weeks based on our current technology, one hundred years ago viability was much later in pregnancy, and likely in one hundred years, it will be much earlier. Whether or not someone can survive outside of their natural environment does not tell us if they are living. It simply tells us whether or not we have the technology to care for them if they are outside of this natural environment. Finally, in order to ask the question, "Can they *survive?*", we must first acknowledge the fact that they are *living*. The question of viability is a question of survival—thus, it presumes that life has already begun, and asks whether or not it might end. We would not speak of viability unless we are speaking of a being that is already alive.[14]

---

14   This way of addressing the *vitality vs. viability* argument was presented by Blaise Alleyne.

2.6 It's a baby!

It is important to note that while in the earliest stages of development an embryo may not have the physical characteristics we attribute to human beings, this changes very quickly. With the incredible leaps in embryology and the visibility of the embryo and fetus through increasingly sophisticated technologies such as the ultrasound, it is shocking how little knowledge there is surrounding pre-natal development. The pro-choice movement has so effectively monopolized the debate that most people truly believe that pre-born children are merely clumps of cells, completely unidentifiable as human beings until months into pregnancy. This, abortion advocates claim, is true at least through the first trimester and quite far into the second. After those stages, according to them, abortions are obtained only for very serious reasons, such as when the life of the mother and/or child are at risk. As such, what could be wrong with evicting a blob of tissue from your body?

The truth that pre-born children are identifiably human quite early in pregnancy is not our first line of defense. Abortion would be wrong even if this was not true. What the embryo and fetus look like does not change the fact that they are living human beings. However, it can be helpful in conversation to be aware of some basic embryology facts. While people may try to contradict any information we present on pre-natal development, information is easily accessible via smartphone, and we can use on-the-spot web searches to prove the validity of our claims.

Because not everyone has access to an embryology textbook, the website *The Endowment for Human Development* (ehd.org) is a very helpful resource to use in conversation. Here is a list of facts that, once committed to memory, can be useful tools in discussions about abortion:

- **The brain is the first organ to appear. At 3 weeks the three primary sections of the brain can be identified.**

- **At 3 weeks and 1 day after fertilization, the heart begins to beat.** This is important information, as many women do not even know that they are pregnant at this point, which means that an abortion—barring abortions caused by abortifacient birth control and the morning after pill— nearly always stops a beating heart.

- **At 6 weeks, the external ear is developing.** External characteristics that we often associate with being human are developing very early on.

- **Brainwaves have been detected at 6 weeks and 2 days.** Knowing this is important, as many say that the embryo and fetus are not conscious because they don't have a brain. The fact is that the brain is present and beginning to function already in the first trimester, though consciousness has not yet developed.

- **Taste buds begin to form on the tongue and the pre-born child can hiccup at just 7 weeks.**

- **At 8 weeks, if all is well, each tiny hand has five separate fingers, and each foot has five toes.** When one sees an image of an abortion victim, one of the most jarring sights is the tiny hands and feet of the child, so clearly human despite his or her small size.

- **At just 9 weeks the pre-born child sucks his or her thumb and can grasp an object, as well as stretch. This marks the end of the embryonic period and the beginning of the fetal period.**

- **Tiny fingernails and toenails are present at 10 weeks.**

- **The nose and lips are completely developed at 11 weeks,**

allowing the fetus to have complex facial expressions.[15]

It is very important to note that all of the above developments take place within the first trimester, when the majority of abortions occur. The pre-born child is tiny, but all of the major systems of the body are already in place, and the baby is very obviously just that: a growing human baby.

2.7 In Practice

The science of when life begins may seem complicated at first, and it can be easy to become overwhelmed. While it is good to have a general understanding of the science of when life begins, our most important tool is the human rights argument. Using the human rights argument in conversation is nearly always straightforward. There are two ways that these questions are typically used. The first is when the conversation begins with discussing difficult circumstances. This means that we have already **bridged the conversational gap** and reached the point where someone has said that they do not believe a pre-born child is a human being in the same way that a born child is. That type of conversation often looks something like this:

A. After Bridging the Gap

Imagine you have asked a young woman the **question:** *"If we may not kill a born child because of a difficult situation, why may we kill a pre-born child because of the same situation?"*

And she has replied: "Because that's different."

---

15   All of these facts come from: Moore, Persaud, Torchia, *The Developing Human: Clinically Oriented Embryology, 7th edition.* Philadelphia, PA: Elsevier, 2003. pgs. 85 and 103, as well as: "Prenatal Form and Function—The Making of an Earth Suit," The Endowment For Human Development. Accessed February 7, 2018. http://www.ehd.org/dev_article_unit4.php.

"How so?" you ask.

"Because it's not really a human being."

"I see what you're saying. I was just wondering: **if two human beings reproduce, what will their offspring be?**"

"What do you mean?"

"Well, dogs have dogs and cats have cats, right?"

"Yeah . . ."

"So what do human beings have?"

She rolls her eyes. "Human beings, obviously."

"Right! And **if something is growing, isn't it alive?**"

"Yeah, I guess that makes sense."

"And **do you believe in human rights?**"

"Of course I do!"

"Great! Me too," you reply, quickly establishing **common ground**. "The question I have then, is that if two human beings can only reproduce another human being, and if we know that something is alive when it is growing, then **doesn't it logically follow that abortion is a human rights violation?**"

"Wow, I never thought of it that way. That definitely gives me something to think about."

Often the final response to this type of conversation is like the fictional response of our imaginary young woman. However, she might have said, *"Well, it's just a fetus!"* or, *"But it isn't really an actual life yet."* In those cases, the conversation would continue with these questions: **"What**

kind of fetus?" or, **"Would you agree with me that life can begin at one of three points: before, at, or sometime after fertilization?"** The most important thing to remember here is that we can continually remind the person we are speaking with that they believe in human rights, and science tells us that human life begins at the moment of fertilization. This means that (by their own admission), abortion must be a human rights violation.

Testimony Spotlight

"Hello, what do you think about abortion?" I asked a young man walking by.

"I don't really know. I guess if it's a baby, abortion is wrong. But we don't really know when life begins, do we?" He grinned. "It's probably something I should be thinking about, though. I'm studying pre-nursing at the moment."

"That's a great question! Would you agree with me that life can only begin at one of three points: before fertilization, at fertilization, or at some point after fertilization?"

He thought for a moment and then nodded. "That makes sense."

"Can a sperm left alone in a man's body, or an egg left alone in a woman's ever grow and develop into a mature human being?"

"Nope, it doesn't work that way!"

"Right, so we know that life can't begin before fertilization. Let's take some point after fertilization.

Testimony Spotlight - *continued*

Do doctors bring us babies in their black bags?"

He laughed. "Okay, I see where you're going with this."

"Obviously not," I agreed. "We know that infants grew and developed from younger versions of themselves, fetuses. And do pregnant women wake up in the middle of the night with a fetus moving and kicking inside of them?"

"Nope, they were embryos first."

"Right, and where does the embryo come from?"

"Ummm . . . Fertilization?"

"Right! Science tells us that at the moment of fertilization, a whole, distinct, living human being comes into existence."

"That really makes sense!" He agreed. We talked for little longer about how important it is to know how to explain why abortion is wrong, particularly in the medical field. **Before he left, he thanked me for talking with him, agreeing that abortion is a human rights violation.**

~ Meagan Vande Bruinhorst

B. I don't really know

The second type of conversation that we use the human rights argument in, is when the conversation begins with someone saying that they don't really know what they think about abortion. These conversations look something like this:

"Hello," you say, offering a teenage boy a pamphlet. "What do you think about abortion?"

"I don't really know," he answers. "I haven't given it much thought."

"That's fair," you reply. "**Do you believe in human rights?**"

"Yeah, I do," he says, nodding his head for extra emphasis.

"Great, me too! And **who do you think should get human rights?**"

He looks confused. "That's kind of a weird question. Uh, human beings?"

"Of course, that's common sense, isn't it? Human beings have human rights. And **if someone's parents are human, we know that they're human too, right?** As in, human beings can only reproduce human beings?"

"Yeah, human beings have human beings."

"Well, if human beings can only have human beings, and we believe in human rights for *all* human beings, **then doesn't that mean that abortion is a human rights violation?**"

"Um . . . Okay, I totally see what you're saying. But is the baby even alive?"

"Well, **if something is growing, isn't it alive?** If the embryo or fetus wasn't growing, why would a woman need an abortion?"

"Good point. When you put it that way, it *does* look like abortion is a human rights violation!"

Again, the conversation could go further. Sometimes at this point someone brings up a difficult circumstance that the woman might be facing, and you can show through questions that we don't kill human beings because of problems; we seek to eliminate suffering, not eliminate sufferers.

Testimony Spotlight

"Hi!" I greeted a man walking by. "What do you think about abortion?"

"Oh, it's totally irresponsible," he replied. "We ought to be willing to accept the consequences of what we do. I do think it's necessary in certain circumstances, though."

"I agree that there are many difficult circumstances a woman can find herself in. However, would we ever kill a newborn who was in those circumstances?" I asked.

"No," he told me.

"Then why would we kill a pre-born child in the same difficult circumstances?"

He acknowledged that it depended on when life begins. We discussed the science of when life begins and before he left he said: "Thank you for this new information! **Life begins at fertilization and we should try to stop abortion.**"

~ Devorah Gilman

2.8 Conclusion

Every step of a conversation brings new challenges. What the human rights argument teaches us is that we need to have an understanding of the science of how and when life begins if we want to be able to communicate our position well. The pro-life position is a simple one, and the science to back it up is also simple to understand. We do not need a degree in biology to understand that life begins at fertilization. This argument is very powerful for several reasons. The first is that it emphasizes something that nearly everyone has in common: a belief in fundamental human rights. We may be of different religions and different ethnic backgrounds, but human rights are something that most of us can agree on. The human rights argument helps us reach people where they are at. The second is that it is both easy to understand and easy to articulate. Initially, many people believe that the pro-life position does not have a leg to stand on. When we are confident in the use of the human rights argument, and people exclaim: "You're ridiculous!" We may reply, as always, with a question: "Could you tell me, please, what is ridiculous about believing that human rights belong to every living human being, and that those rights begin when the human being begins?" The position is clear. However, there are people who attempt to muddy the waters even after this point. Dealing with the questions they have requires us to delve into a little philosophy.

Key Takeaways

- The fundamental question of the abortion debate is: *What are the pre-born?*

- This question can be answered through the **Human Rights Argument**:

  1. *Do you believe in human rights?*

  2. *Who should have human rights?*

  3. *If two human beings reproduce, what will their offspring be?*

  4. *If something is growing, isn't it alive?*

- The words *embryo* and *fetus* are age classifications in the same way that infant, toddler, and teenager are age classifications. They don't tell us *what something* is, they simply tell us *how old someone* is.

- When does life begin? This question can be answered by going through the points:

  - *before fertilization*

  - *at fertilization*, or

  - *at some point after fertilization.*

2.9 Diving Deeper

1. The only question that needs to be answered in the abortion debate is: *What are the pre-born?* Why is this the only question that matters? Is it possible that this question could eventually become challenged? How?

2. Why is the idea of human rights so important? What could a society that does not subscribe to human rights look like?

3. Is it logically possible to argue that life begins at a point other than fertilization? How might people try to explain themselves when arguing that our lives *did not* begin at fertilization?

2.10 Suggested Activities

1. Many people believe that a pre-born child is just a clump of cells until the third trimester of pregnancy. Visit the website *The Endowment for Human Development* (ehd.org). What facts can you present that disprove this idea? Memorize at least three of them.

2. With a partner, go through the human rights argument. Have your friend pretend to be pro-choice. After your friend has told you that they don't know what they think about abortion, use the human rights argument to lead them to the pro-life position. Then switch and give your friend a turn to practice.

3. Research different endangered species. What measures are taken to protect these species? Is there ever a time when certain members of a species are protected while others are not?

2.11 Additional Resources

- *Pro-Life 101*, by Scott Klusendorf

  - This booklet gives a good summary of the foundational arguments of the pro-life movement, with additional tips on how to share this information in different settings.

- "When Does Human Life Begin?", an essay by Maureen Condic

  - This paper can be downloaded here: https://bdfund. org/wp-content/uploads/2016/05/wi_whitepaper_ life_print.pdf. It gives a comprehensive explanation as to why the scientific community believes life begins at fertilization.

- *The Endowment for Human Development* website (ehd.org)

  - Understanding basic pre-natal development is valuable. This website provides facts, images, videos, timelines, and much more to illustrate a child's development in the womb.

Part Three: Personhood

Who do human rights belong to?

"We can argue forever what personhood means, but there is no empirical or logical way to prove it. It's the beginning of the argument, not the endpoint."
The Wizard of Oz

3.1 Introduction

"I think I have some questions that you've never thought of before." The young man in front of me smiled condescendingly.

"Well," I replied, "I always appreciate hearing new points of view. Let's hear it."

He folded his arms and shook back his blonde curls. Ontario's early summer humidity had made it frizzy, and it kept falling over his eyes.

"You have to understand," he began, "that the question is not whether fetuses are *human*."

"Oh no?" I asked.

"No. Being *human* really doesn't mean anything." He paused significantly.

"Oh no?" I said again.

"Shall I tell you what does matter?" I had a feeling he was going to tell me whether I wanted him to or not, but I nodded to hear him out.

"Personhood." He announced triumphantly. "Fetuses aren't persons, and so they don't have rights."

"Okay," I said. "I see what you're saying. Just to clarify, what do you think makes a person a person?"

"Consciousness." He declared firmly. "If you can't even think, feel, and suffer, you are not a person. Fetuses are *potential persons*, but they are not real persons. Women are persons, and so their rights must *always* come first."

Fortunately, this philosophical young man was wrong. I

had heard this argument before, and, much to his annoyance, I had a ready answer. To play with the concept of personhood as a mind game is one thing, but when translated to real life, there can be no real winner.

3.2 What makes a person a person?

The **human rights argument** is an effective tool, but it isn't always enough to convince others that human rights belong to the pre-born as well. Pro-choice academics have recognized the conflict between abortion and human rights since the very beginning. To counter the human rights argument, they set out to develop an explanation as to why human rights do not necessarily belong to this particular group of human beings. The concept they use to muddy the waters of reason is not a new one. It is the same idea used throughout history to enable the strong to prey on the weak: the concept of legal personhood. "Yes," they agree, nodding wisely, "you are correct. The fetus *is* a human being. However, it is not a person. *Persons* are those beings which are valuable to the extent that we bestow upon them fundamental human rights." While this statement may make us upset, we may not forget the simple conversational tactics taught in Part One. In this case, we answer again with a **question**.

A. *SLED*

When someone explains that the pre-born are not persons, the first question we should ask is a clarifying one: "What do you think a person is?" We will receive varying answers, and as will be emphasized later in this section, this variability is the greatest weakness of the personhood-denying argument. Ultimately, the answers people give fit into four different categories. Stephen Schwarz, in his book

The Moral Question of Abortion, arranged these categories into the acronym *SLED:*[1]

Size

Level of Development

Environment

Degree of Dependence

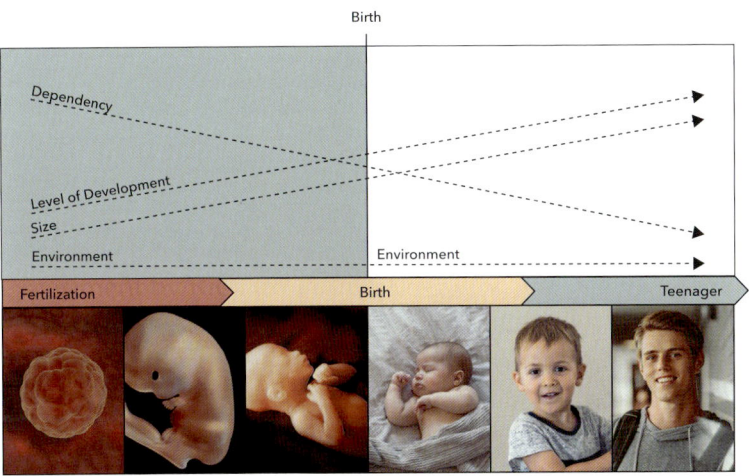

Figure 3.1 *SLED*

For example, when asked: "What do you think makes a person a person?" someone might reply: "A fetus isn't a person because it is in a woman's body." This refers to the **environment** of the pre-born child. Another might say: "A fetus can't think or feel." A fetus may not think or feel

---

1   Stephen Schwarz, *The Moral Question of Abortion* (Chicago: Loyola University Press, 1990), 17.

because of his or her **level of development**. When a person declares: "But the baby can't survive on its own, it needs to get all of its nutrients from the mother," they are referring to the child's **degree of dependency**. Finally, someone might mention that the embryo and fetus are much smaller than we are, and this emphasizes the importance of a human being's **size** in relation to personhood. If all that is necessary is a simple illustration, we need only show that these four categories exist on a continuum. Our size, level of development, environment, and degree of dependency are constantly changing. These four categories help differentiate between a fetus and infant, but also between an infant and toddler, and a toddler and adolescent. Once again, we may emphasize the question: **"If these things don't matter *after* birth, why do they matter *before* birth?"**

Testimony Spotlight

"It's inside a woman's body. It depends on her completely, so she should have the choice to have an abortion if she wants to," the young man told me.

"It's true that the pre-born child is completely dependent on his or her mother for food, water, and a safe environment. Would you agree with me, though, that newly born infants are completely dependent on their caregivers for the same kinds of support?"

"Yeah, I guess that's true," he admitted, after thinking for a moment.

Testimony Spotlight - *continued*

"Should a mother or caregiver be allowed to abandon or kill their born child if they were unable to care for that child anymore?" I asked.

"Oh. I see where you're coming from."

"Don't you agree, then, that if the pre-born are human beings they should still have human rights, even if they're dependent on their mothers?"

"**Yes. Yes, that makes sense**," he agreed.

~ Cameron Côté

3.3 Sentience

Again, pro-choice thinkers have anticipated our reply. They too realize that the things that make adults different from fetuses are the same things that make adults different from toddlers. The same factors used to justify ending the lives of fetuses do not, in their reasoning, translate over to toddlers. This fact necessitates a better defense of the pro-choice personhood argument: Enter sentience. While we encounter different opinions on what makes a person a person, what we will likely hear most often is something like this: "It's not a person because it isn't conscious," "It isn't even aware of its own existence," "A fetus doesn't have any experiences," "It isn't sentient," or "The fetus can't think, it doesn't know anything." Essentially, the argument is that an entity that has no thoughts, desires or even knowledge of its own existence cannot be classified as a person, or at least is not valuable enough to justify overriding a "woman's right to choose."

A. Amoebas and Embryos

First, it is important to expose what this argument is really saying. The idea of sentience fits into the **level of development** category. An embryo or fetus is not conscious only because they have not yet reached a certain stage of development. The key word here is *yet.* Our level of development is reflected in our age. Therefore, at their earliest stages human beings are not conscious, but this is only because they are young. To illustrate this point, we can use a helpful analogy.[2] Imagine you are speaking with a philosophy student who has just told you that they believe that in order to be a person we must have consciousness.

"Okay," you say, "I see what you're saying, I just want to clarify something. Imagine that you are holding an amoeba in one hand and a single-celled embryo in the other."

"Exactly," the philosophy student interrupts excitedly. "An amoeba and a single-celled embryo have the same level of function, and yet we don't protect amoebas!"

"Is the amoeba conscious?" you ask.

"No, it isn't."

"Will it ever be conscious?"

"No, obviously not."

"Why will the amoeba never be conscious?"

Now the student is becoming slightly annoyed. "Because it's an amoeba! It is not in its nature to be a conscious thing."

"Exactly," you reply. "Now what about the embryo? Is the embryo conscious?"

---

2   Stephanie Gray, *Love Unleashes Life* (Toronto: Life Cycle Books, 2016), 47-48.

"No. I already told you that it has the same level of functioning as the amoeba!"

"Right. But *why* isn't the embryo conscious?"

"Because it hasn't developed a brain yet."

"And why hasn't it developed a brain yet?"

The student does an exaggerated eye-roll. "Because it hasn't had the time!"

"Interesting," you say. "The embryo isn't conscious because it hasn't developed a brain—because it hasn't had the time. Time is reflected in our age, isn't it? So, aren't we just saying that those of us who are older may kill those of us who are younger?"

"What do you mean?" he says, confused.

"Well, the amoeba can't think because of *what* it is, while the embryo can't think because of *how old* she is. When we say that one must be conscious in order to be a person, we are saying that those of us who are older are more valuable than those who are younger."

Framing the debate around *age-based discrimination* or *ageism* is very important. In our society, we recognize that discriminating against people based on arbitrary characteristics about themselves that they cannot change is wrong. Just as someone cannot change their skin colour or their ethnicity, one cannot change their age. As Randy Alcorn points out, "Age, size, IQ, or stage of development are simply differences in degree, not in kind . . . none of these make some people better or more human than others. None make some qualified to live, and others unqualified."[3]

---

3   Randy Alcorn, *ProLife Answers to ProChoice Arguments* (Portland: Multnomah Press, 1992), 57.

B. Functionalism

Essentially, the sentience argument is a functionalist argument, championed by philosophers such as Dr. Peter Singer. Functionalism places value on the presence of a certain *function*, i.e. sentience, rather than on an entity's *nature*. Singer's qualifications for personhood dictates that one must have an "awareness of existence over time in different places with the capacity to have wants and plans for the future."[4] According to this definition, embryos, fetuses, and even infants cannot be considered persons. In fact, Singer claims that an adult pig is more sentient, and therefore more deserving of personhood status, than a newborn human being.[5]

Functionalism claims that in order to *be* a person, we must first *function* as a person. What functionalism often fails to address is that if this were the case, human beings could gain and lose personhood status periodically throughout their lives. They would lose this status, for example, when they go under general anesthetic or if they are comatose. It is more logical to suggest that in order to *function* as a person, we must first *be* a person. To explain this idea, it is again helpful to use an analogy:

*Many people find it difficult to tell the difference between tortoises and turtles. The most important difference between the two is that tortoises live on land and turtles spend most or all of their time in water. If, upon encountering one of these creatures, you want to see which it is, you could place it in water and see what happens. If the animal begins to swim, you know that what you have discovered is a turtle. However, the turtle did not become a turtle when it began to swim—or, in other words, when it began to **function** as a turtle. The turtle always **was** a turtle, by nature a swimming creature. The*

---

4   Peter Singer, *Practical Ethics* (Cambridge: Cambridge University Press, 1990), 51, 76, cited in CCBR's previous pro-life classroom.

5   Peter Singer, *Practical Ethics* (Cambridge: Cambridge University Press, 1997), 169-171., cited in Scott Klusendorf's Biola document.

function did not make the turtle a turtle. **The fact that the turtle was a turtle allowed it to function as one.**[6]

Essentially, it is our nature that makes us who we are, not how we function. The sentience argument claims that a preborn child would not be considered a person because she does not have an **immediately exercisable capacity** for sentience. It is important to note that an embryo does have the **inherent capacity** for sentience, as part of her human nature. **The only difference between having an inherent capacity and having an immediately exercisable capacity is time.**

The functionalism argument is not only deeply flawed. It is dangerous, as it bases rights on subjective opinion. If we choose to value function over nature, the debates begin. Which functions ought we to consider valuable? Once we settle on a function, we must then decide at what point this function truly manifests itself. For example, one might base human value on brain function. However, is this value conferred at the moment brain waves are first detected? Advanced technology reveals that brain waves are being discovered at earlier and earlier gestations. Does this mean that brain function is only valuable if it is detectable by the technology we have at present? Are we placing value on specific functions of the brain or on the brain as a whole? When we start placing value on accidental attributes rather than on substance, the number of questions that follow are infinite.

Not only is there an unlimited amount of questions when we adhere to a doctrine of functionalism, there is also an unlimited number of answers. This observation is significant, particularly because as a society we recognize the danger of basing public policy on subjective opinions. We may have differing ideas on what makes human beings valuable, but we cannot debate the scientific fact that human life begins at

---

6   This analogy was presented during a CCBR internship pro-life 201 training.

fertilization. The question we must ask is, What should public policy be based on? Subjective opinion or scientific fact? As Jonathon Van Maren points out, the so-called philosophies of pro-choice advocates are "subjective, fickle, and inconsistent."[7] Scientific fact, on the other hand, is neither subjective nor fickle. This observation is reiterated by Michelle Hauser in an article published in the National Post. The scientific advancements of medicine and embryology, she claims, "will drag us, kicking and screaming . . . into the public square for a good old-fashioned barn-burner of a debate." Further, "Head-in-sand will no longer be an option for any government or its electorate. . . How remarkable it will be when science forces us to have a debate that politics had apparently put to rest."[8]

C. Speciesism

If one espouses the sentient/functionalist argument, it naturally follows that such a person would be against what is called speciesism. Dr. Peter Singer argues that sentience is the only logical, non-arbitrary point at which to confer personhood, writing:

> If a being is not capable of suffering, or of experiencing enjoyment or happiness, there is nothing to be taken into account. This is why the limit of sentience (using the term as a convenient, if not strictly accurate, shorthand for the capacity to suffer or experience enjoyment or happiness) is the only defensible boundary of concern for the interests of others.[9]

---

7   Jonathon Van Maren, "Banning abortion is just science-based public policy, " endthekilling.ca, July 19, 2016, accessed November 28, 2017.

8   Michelle Hauser, "Pro-life debates, with a sci-fi twist," nationalpost.com, June 30, 2016, http://nationalpost.com/opinion/michelle-hauser-pro-life-debates-with-a-sci-fi-twist.

9   Peter Singer, "All Animals Are Equal," colorado.edu (1974): 4-5. http://spot.colorado.edu/~heathwoo/phil1200,Spr07/singer.pdf.

Testimony Spotlight

While doing pro-life outreach, I spoke to a woman who said that one of her family members had had an abortion because they were told that their baby had disabilities. I told her that I was sorry for her family's loss, and then told her about my friend's sister, who has developmental challenges.

"Would it be okay for my friend to end her sister's life because she can't function in the same way that people without disabilities can?" I asked gently.

"Of course not!" she exclaimed, horrified.

"Would you say that a disabled person is less human, and therefore should be given human rights only *based on what they can or cannot do?*"

She thought for a minute and then said: "**What you're saying makes total sense. Abortion is always wrong, and I'm going to show this brochure to my family**." She smiled at me. "Thank you for being out here today, I've never heard this perspective before."

~ Yvonne Struck

If sentience is the limit chosen, then certain human beings will fall outside the limit, and certain animals will fall within it, meaning that in order to be inclusive of other species, we will be exclusive within our own. In fact, Singer argues that it is not logical that rights "[include] infants and even mental defectives,"[10] and exclude sentient beings that he claims are

---

10   Peter Singer, "All Animals Are Equal," colorado.edu (1974): 4-5. http://spot.colorado.edu/~heathwoo/phil1200,Spr07/singer.pdf.

more able to suffer. Those who focus on human rights as belonging to all members of the species *homo sapiens,* are what he calls speciesist, explaining the concept this way:

> The racist violates the principle of equality by giving greater weight to the interests of members of his own race, when there is a clash between their interests and interests of those of another race. Similarly the speciesist allows the interests of his own species to override the greater interests of members of other species.[11]

There are several problems with this way of thinking. First, it is natural for members of a species to put the interests of their species first. After all, if someone saw a baby and a pig about to be hit by a car, wouldn't they choose to save the child? Moreover, Singer's own reasoning espouses speciesism in a certain sense; if advanced functioning confers value, does it not make logical sense to place higher value on the species that has created computers and has landed on the moon? As Stephanie Gray pointed out:

> "a human may not *currently* have impressive abilities, but by virtue of *being* human, an individual *inherently* has impressive abilities. For while a dog's ability to cure disease is *not ever,* a human baby's ability to cure disease is *not yet.*"[12]

Secondly, Singer's claim that putting the interests of human beings first causes harm to other species does not hold up under more serious examination. It is true that a discussion about the rights of animals could prove to be valuable. Human beings have a responsibility to care for other creatures and may not exploit them or cause them to suffer unnecessarily.

---

11   Peter Singer, "All Animals Are Equal," colorado.edu (1974): 4-5. http://spot.colorado.edu/~heathwoo/phil1200,Spr07/singer.pdf.

12   Stephanie Gray wrote this in CCBR's previous online pro-life classroom.

However, the comparison between animal rights and human rights is problematic for several reasons. First, while it is true that in Singer's definition, certain animals are more sentient than pre-born children and even infants, the problem here is the functionalism problem. The pre-born child is not sentient because he/she is not old enough to have developed that function. Therefore, in saying that an infant is not entitled to human rights until they are sentient, we are engaging in age-based discrimination, or ableism.

Further, the pro-life argument does not claim that animals should not have rights, it simply claims that *all* human beings are entitled to human rights and must be protected from discrimination. For example, we may debate the rights of animals, but if we decide that a species must be protected, would it not be logical to protect all members of that group? As outlined in Part One, *Protecting a Species,* if we are protecting bald eagles, we wouldn't protect only the adult eagles, we would protect *every* eagle, regardless of the animal's age.

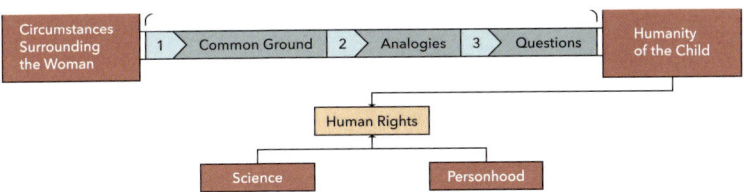

Figure 3.2 *It all comes back to human rights — Credit: this image was created by Blaise Alleyne.*

3.4 The strong against the weak

The danger of basing human rights on the subjective idea of personhood is not new. Throughout history, separating personhood from humanity was a tactic used to allow a certain group of people to oppress another group. In 1858, the Virginia Supreme Court declared that, "In the eyes of the

Clarifying Terms

"It's a parasite!"

In some ways, dehumanization is subtle, but in one of the most transparently dehumanizing tactics, pre-born children are labelled as parasites. Because pre-born children "attach themselves" to their mothers and "feed off them," the reasoning goes, they are simply a form of parasite. (Again, this is nothing new. Jewish people were portrayed as rats on Nazi propaganda posters, and Hutu extremists labelled Tutsis as cockroaches during the Rwandan genocide.) In order to refute this claim, we need to turn to the definition of parasite. The literal definition of the word is defined by the Merriam-Webster dictionary as "an organism living in, with, or on another organism in parasitism," with parasitism being defined as "an intimate association between organisms of two or more kinds; especially: one in which a parasite obtains benefits from a host which it usually injures."

It is important to note that first of all, a parasite is of a different kind or species than its host. Furthermore, the relationship between a parasite and its host is usually harmful, and as such, unnatural. Being invaded by parasites is unhealthy, keeping the body from functioning properly, while pregnancy is a clear sign that the body is functioning in the way that it should. Additionally, there is some evidence that rather than pregnancy being a harmful relationship between mother and child, it is a mutually beneficial relationship.

Clarifying Terms - *continued*

Pregnancy and childbirth may guard against breast cancer, as it has been discovered that a baby's fetal cells appear more in a mother's healthy breast tissue and less frequently in a woman suffering from breast cancer *[Doucleff, Michaeleen. "Fetal cells may protect mom from disease long after the baby's born," (Oct. 26, 2015). https://www.npr.org/sections/health-shots/2015/10/26/449966350/fetal-cells-may-protect-mom-from-disease-long-after-the-babys-born].*

By definition, a pre-born child is not a parasite: fetuses are not invading organisms, they are not evidence of improper bodily function, and they are not in a harmful relationship with their mother. Calling pre-born children parasites is yet another dehumanization tactic that needs to be entirely rejected.

law . . . the slave is not a person."[13] This thinking justified white plantation owners in their enslavement of African Americans. In many situations, First Nations peoples were also treated horrifically. An American Law Review in 1881 stated that, "An Indian is not a person within the meaning of the Constitution,"[14] thus justifying their actions. The fight for women's rights played out differently throughout the Western world, but initially the goal was the same: to be viewed with respect, and to be viewed as persons. After all, the British Voting Rights case of 1909 declared that, "The

13   Bailey v. Poindexter's Executor (1858), Virginia Supreme Court, cited in the National Post: http://nationalpost.com/news/canada/brandon-university-students-for-life.

14   George Canfield, American Law Review (1881), cited in the National Post.

statutory word 'person' did not in these circumstances include women."[15] Finally, the separation of personhood from humanity was used as justification for one of the most recognizable tragedies of our time: the Holocaust. A German Supreme Court decision of 1936 reads, "The Reichsgericht itself refused to recognize Jews . . . as 'persons' in the legal sense."[16]

In light of these histories, Jonathon Van Maren posits an important question: **"Name one time in human history when the phrase 'legal personhood' was used to include or protect a group of people."**[17] The answer to this question is, quite simply, never. The only instances throughout history in which human beings have separated the terms humanity and personhood were with the purpose of *including* themselves and *excluding* others. This gave them the authority to treat other groups of human beings as they saw fit. So, the bloody history of "legal personhood" has repeated itself, over and over, until today, in which the Canadian Supreme Court declared in 1997 that, **"The law of Canada does not recognize the unborn child as a legal person possessing rights."**[18]

The danger of basing human rights on the concept of personhood has not always escaped notice. The Universal Declaration of Human Rights was adopted in December of 1948. In conversation, it is often effective to ask people, "What is significant about the year 1948?" Many recognize this date as being shortly after the end of World War II. "And what happened," we may ask, "during World War

15   British Voting Rights case (1909), cited in the National Post.

16   German Supreme Court decision (1936), cited in the National Post.

17   Jonathon Van Maren, "The shockingly bloody history of 'legal personhood'," *LifeSite News*, February 19, 2015, https://www.lifesitenews.com/blogs/the-shockingly-bloody-history-of-legal-personhood.

18   Canadian Supreme Court, Winnipeg Child and Family Services Case (1997), National Post, http://nationalpost.com/news/canada/brandon-university-students-for-life.

II, that, when revealed, had the world reeling in shock?" What we are referring to, of course, is the Holocaust. Nazi Germany justified killing those they saw as unfit to live by denying them personhood under the law, thus stripping them of their fundamental human rights. In light of this knowledge, it is significant to note that the first lines of the Universal Declaration of Human Rights' preamble read: ". . . [the] recognition of the inherent dignity and of the equal and inalienable rights of **all members of the human family** is the foundation of freedom, justice and peace in the world . . ." (emphasis added).[19]

The phrase: "all members of the human family," is important. It is an indisputable fact that pre-born children are human beings, and thus are part of this family. Further, the Canadian Charter of Rights and Freedoms declares in article 7 that, "Everyone has the right to life, liberty and security of the person and the right not to be deprived thereof except in accordance with the principles of fundamental justice." Further, article 15 states that, "Every individual is equal before and under the law and has the right to equal protection and equal benefit of the law without discrimination and, in particular, without discrimination based on race, national or ethnic origin, colour, religion, sex, **age**, or mental or physical disability" (emphasis added).[20] These documents clearly support the human rights argument. The pre-born are members of the human family and therefore have the right to life: Fundamental rights cannot be denied them because of their lack of development or dependence, as that is age-based discrimination (ageism).

---

19   Universal Declaration of Human Rights, Preamble, *United Nations,* http://www.un.org/en/udhrbook/pdf/udhr_booklet_en_web.pdf.

20   The Canadian Charter of Rights and Freedoms, accessed here: http://laws-lois.justice.gc.ca/eng/Const/page-15.html.

Testimony Spotlight

"Hi!" I greeted a university student walking by. "What do you think about abortion?"

"Fetuses don't get human rights," he responded.

"If the pre-born are human beings," I asked him, "then how do we have the right to deny them their human rights?"

"Well, they're still inside a woman's body, completely dependent on her for their survival."

"Okay," I said. "Just a question: Throughout history, we've denied human beings *their* human rights based on race, ethnicity, gender, and other arbitrary characteristics. Why would age or dependency be any different?"

He opened his mouth and then shut it again. He gave me a sheepish grin and said, "When you put it that way, I can't deny that your logic makes total sense."

~ Jonathon Van Maren

3.5 In Practice

Discussing personhood may seem intimidatingly philosophical, but when we recognize how closely related this argument is to the **human rights argument,** it isn't as difficult as it first appears. Every conversation can be tied back to how all human beings ought to have human rights, regardless of age. Any argument against personhood for the pre-born is inherently discrimination based on age or ability.

A. *Sentience*

"You mentioned you were a public speaker," the hairdresser says, busily shampooing your hair. "What do you speak about?"

You groan inwardly—you were hoping to avoid this conversation for once. But, knowing you're not supposed to avoid opportunities when they arise, you answer, "Pro-life issues. What do you think about abortion?"

Her hands go still for a moment and you know that she feels as trapped as you do. "Well, I think that as long as fetuses can't think or suffer like we can, abortion is totally a woman's choice."

"I agree, they can't think like we can."

Before you can continue, she jumps in eagerly. "Exactly! If they can't feel or think, then they don't have rights in the same way that we do."

"Okay, I see what you're saying. Why can't they think?"

"Sorry?" She has begun rinsing your hair now, and you wonder ruefully if she sprayed water down your neck on purpose.

"Why can't a fetus think?" you repeat, patiently.

"Well, I guess because it doesn't have a brain."

"Right, and why doesn't it have a brain?"

"I'm not really sure where you're going with this," she says, reaching for the conditioner, "but I guess it's because they haven't had the time to develop one yet."

"Interesting. The fetus can't think because it hasn't had the time to develop a brain yet. Isn't time reflected in our age?"

"Yes . . ."

"Then aren't we just saying that those of us who are older are allowed to kill those of us who are younger?"

"Well . . . Repeat that?"

"A fetus doesn't have a brain because she hasn't had the time to develop one. If she is given more time, she'll be able to think and feel like the rest of us. The only real difference between the person you are now and the fetus that you once were is time. You're older now."

"Oh. I see what you're saying." She wraps a towel around your head.

"Wouldn't you agree, then, that saying that abortion is okay based on what a fetus can do is essentially age-based discrimination?"

"When you put it that way, that's totally true!"

This conversation could have been approached in several different ways, but keeping it simple, asking a lot of questions, and focusing on proving that abortion is **age-based discrimination** will serve you well.

B. *Human Rights Documents*

"Hello, **do you believe in human rights**?" you ask a man walking by.

"Yes, yes I do," he says, stopping in his tracks.

"Great, me too! **Who do you think should have human rights**?"

He smiles shrewdly. "People. Only those who are considered persons are entitled to human rights."

"Interesting. I'm just curious, have you ever heard of the **UN Declaration of Human Rights**?"

"Of course I have!" He exclaims, slightly offended that you even asked.

"Great! So, I assume you know when it was written?"

"You may have me there," he says with a grin. "Some time after World War II, I'm pretty sure."

"You're right, the year was 1948. Of course, at this point the world was beginning to understand the horrific extent of the Holocaust."

"Right. Where are you going with this?"

"Well, the UN Declaration of Human Rights' preamble states that human rights belong to **every member of the human family.** Why do you think they used language like that?"

For the first time, he actually looks interested. "Enlighten me."

"Well, the Nazis justified murdering millions of Jews, because they said that while they may be some sort of human, they were not considered persons in the legal sense. When we understand the context, isn't it significant that the UN Declaration used the phrase 'every member of the human family?'"

"Okay, I think I hear what you're saying."

"After the Holocaust we realized that separating the words person and human being was a dangerous thing to do. We realized that the only way to protect all human beings was not to focus on the subjective idea of personhood, but rather the objective science of humanity. **If two human** beings reproduce, what will their offspring be?"

"Human, obviously."

"Right. And if we believe in human rights for every member of the human family, **doesn't it logically follow that abortion is a human rights violation?**"

He grins and reaches to shake your hand. "Well played. I don't think I can counter that kind of logic."

It's hard to overemphasize the importance of weaving the human rights argument throughout your conversations. It's impossible to combat the idea of personhood without showing that the separation of humanity and personhood is a dangerous concept that threatens the safety of us all. As Martin Luther King Jr. stated, *"Injustice anywhere is a threat to justice everywhere."*[21]

---

21   Martin Luther King Jr.'s "Letter from a Birmingham Jail," accessed here: https://www.africa.upenn.edu/Articles_Gen/Letter_Birmingham.html.

3.6 Conclusion

The systematic dehumanization of pre-born children is enabled by the philosophical arguments denying their personhood. It is easy to point out differences between the pre-born and the born: they are smaller, less developed, require a different environment to survive, and are completely dependent. These differences, claims the pro-choice movement, really matter. Because pre-born human beings cannot function in the same way that born humans can, they are easily excluded from the protective umbrella of human rights. These ideas are not new. We have seen throughout history what happens when we exclude certain members of the human family based on characteristics about themselves that they cannot change. It is past time that we take these lessons to heart: **every living human being ought to have human rights, and these rights should begin when the human being begins.** The terms humanity and personhood should never be separated, and, even if they are, human rights are called human rights—not person rights—for a reason. However, the pro-choice rhetoric does not stop there. *"Alright, fetuses are human beings, and it is possible that they are even persons entitled to human rights,"* they may grudgingly admit. *"But none of that really matters, because the pre-born child resides within the body of a woman."* We have all heard the slogan: *It's her body, it's her choice.* How we respond to these arguments can be found in Part 4.

Key Takeaways

• The pro-abortion personhood argument claims that while pre-born children are scientifically *human beings*, they are not *persons*, and therefore are not entitled to fundamental human rights.

• The characteristics that many claim are important fall into four different categories (SLED):

  • *Size*

  • *Level of Development*

  • *Environment*

  • *Degree of Dependency*

• These characteristics change consistently over time. If human beings are excluded based on any of these categories, this is **age-based discrimination** (ageism).

• Basing personhood on **sentience** is a form of **functionalism**, which means that we do not value human beings based on **what they are**, but rather on **what they can do**.

• The only difference between being able to do something *now* (a one-year old walking), and having the *potential* to do something (a four-month old using their stepping reflex), is time.

• Time is reflected in our age. Therefore, valuing human beings based on what they can do is **ageism**.

3.7 Diving Deeper

1. What do you think are the most important characteristics of a human being? Why? If we based personhood off of these characteristics, would any group of human beings be excluded?

2. What differences can you think of between a pre-born child and yourself? Do these differences influence the way you feel? Are there words and phrases that we and our loved ones use that may contribute to the dehumanization of pre-born children?

3. Is there ever a time where someone or something stronger should be permitted to compromise the rights of someone weaker? What types of situations make this question a difficult one?

3.8 Suggested Activities

1. Read the UN Declaration of Human Rights, The Canadian Charter of Rights and Freedoms, the Declaration of Independence, and the Declaration of the Rights of the Child. What points could be used to defend a right to abortion? What points could be used to defend the rights of pre-born children?

2. Review examples of historical injustice. Can you see evidence of dehumanization? How did the perpetrators of this injustice justify their actions (e.g. the Nuremburg Trials). What is striking about their explanations for their behaviour?

3. With a partner, practice discussing the ideas surrounding personhood. Each partner should take a turn being pro-life and pro-choice. Incorporate SLED, sentience, animal rights, parasitism, and the human rights documents

into your conversation.

3.9 Additional Resources

- *The Moral Question of Abortion,* by Stephen Schwarz

    - This book delves deeply into the philosophical and ethical components of the abortion debate.

- *ProLife Answers to ProChoice Arguments,* by Randy Alcorn

    - This book dismantles pro-choice arguments in an easy to read, question and answer format.

- Life Training Institute (*https://prolifetraining.com*)

    - Life Training Institute offers both articles and videos that dig deeply into the philosophical basis of the pro-choice and pro-life positions. It provides access to live debates where these questions are discussed by experienced pro-life apologists and abortion advocates.

Part Four: It's My Body

No one is allowed to use my body to sustain their life without my permission.

"But the baby which may die because of your choice also has a body. How hard is this to grasp? On the basis of your own argument, the two rights conflict and are irreconcilable."

Peter Hitchens

4.1 Introduction

"Hello," I greeted a middle-aged man walking by. He took a pamphlet from my outstretched hand and flipped it open.

"This is a pro-life pamphlet," he said flatly.

"Yes, sir, it is. What do you think about abortion?"

He ignored my question and looked me up and down. "What I don't understand," he said finally, "is why a young woman like you would be doing something like this."

"Well," I explained, "I believe in human rights for all human beings. **Do you believe in human rights**?"

"No, honey," he said, his tone so patronizing I wanted to scream. "I don't think you understand. Abortion is about *empowering* women. Don't you want to be empowered?"

"I'm sorry, sir," I said—perhaps a little more forcefully than necessary—"but I think it's offensive to suggest that the only way *I* can be equal to *you* is if I have the power to kill my own children."

"Well, umm . . ." He ran a hand through his thinning grey hair. "If you were raped and got pregnant, would you really want to carry that child?"

"It's not so much about what I would *want*," I replied, "as what's *right*. Sexual assault is horrific, I can't imagine what it would be like to suffer through something so traumatic. The question I have for you is, in a country where we don't give the death penalty to the guilty rapist, why do we give it to the innocent child?"

"You're young yet," he said, once again dodging the question. "Are you in university?"

"Yes, I am."

"That's good." He nodded approvingly. "They'll teach you to think more analytically there, instead of with the reactionary mind of a young person."

"How am I responding in a reactionary way?" I asked. "It seems to me that you're the one arguing on the basis of emotion. Logically, if we believe in human rights for all human beings, then, circumstances and women's empowerment aside, abortion *must* be a human rights violation. Correct?"

He was silent for a moment, shifting from one foot to the other. Finally, he glanced up and met my eyes. He gave me a crooked smile and nodded before changing the subject once again: "So, young lady, what are you studying in university?"

4.2 Bodily Autonomy

One of the most recognizable slogans of the pro-choice movement is: "It's my body, it's my choice!" This argument is at the root of pro-choice logic. For many abortion advocates, the humanity and personhood of the pre-born child are irrelevant. They reason that because the pre-born child resides *within* the body of a woman, it is *part* of her body. A pre-born child may be a human being, and may even be entitled to certain rights. However, they argue that the rights of the woman are more important than the rights of the fetus, and therefore she may continue or end her pregnancy as she sees fit. This is known as the **bodily autonomy argument** and it can be approached from several different angles.

Clarifying Terms

The Right to Choose

The pro-choice movement likes to focus on the idea of free choice. In one sense, everyone is pro-choice. People may choose what to wear, what flavour of ice-cream they prefer, or what occupation they wish to pursue. However, in each case being pro-choice completely depends on **what is being chosen**. The claim that everyone has *the right to choose* is an incomplete statement. We cannot discern whether we agree with this statement until we ask: the right to choose what? When someone chooses to break into a neighbour's house, we would recognize this as a bad choice. We all recognize that there are good choices and bad choices; in the case of abortion, the choice is to shred a tiny human being, and this is a choice that we can never support.

A. A hierarchy of rights

In upholding a doctrine of equal human rights, it is inevitable that conflicts of rights will occur. A woman faced with an unwanted pregnancy is in such a situation. She is a human being with human rights, one of which is the **right to bodily autonomy.** Her pre-born child, however, is also a human being entitled to human rights; in this case, **the right to life**. There are two human beings in this case, both with rights that ought to be respected. When cases such as these arise, and rights are in conflict, we always need to uphold the more **fundamental right**. As a society, we recognize that there is a **hierarchy of rights**. For example, the right to bodily autonomy is more important than the right to freedom of expression, and the right to vote is more important than the right to drive.

In a situation where a woman believes that a pregnancy is a threat to her bodily autonomy, pro-choice advocates claim that it is her human right to end that pregnancy. However, since the pre-born child—as a member of the human family who is protected from discrimination based on age—is also entitled to human rights, the answer cannot be so simple. A woman may have a right to bodily autonomy, but a pre-born child is entitled to the right to life. There are two equal human beings' rights that need to be considered. The only choice that we have in this difficult situation is to look at these rights and decide which right is the most important. The right to life is the most important right that we have. Without this right all other rights are redundant; without life we are incapable of enjoying any other liberties that we may have. The right to life must be upheld. This does not assume that the pre-born child is more valuable than the woman, it simply acknowledges the existence of two human beings and treats them without discrimination based on size, level of development, environment, or degree of dependency. Essentially, as Randy Alcorn points out, "The comparison between baby's rights and mother's rights is unequal. What is at stake in abortion is the mother's lifestyle, as opposed to the baby's life."[1]

B. Absolute bodily autonomy

While we may agree that the right to bodily autonomy is a fundamental right, it is important to recognize that this right—along with all other rights—is not absolute. While we recognize the importance of rights, we often pass over the fact that with rights come responsibilities. Along with

---

1   Randy Alcorn, *ProLife Answers to ProChoice Arguments* (Portland: Multnomah Press, 1992), 77.

Testimony Spotlight

"What do you think about abortion?" I asked the university student approaching me.

She paused and then said: "Well, personally I wouldn't have one, but I think it should be every woman's choice what to do with her body."

She was about to leave, so I quickly asked, "What about the baby's body?"

She paused, thinking. Finally she said, "Yeah, I guess I never thought about that before." She took a pamphlet and headed off to class.

~ Nick Rosendal

the right to bodily autonomy, for example, comes the responsibility to respect and protect the bodily autonomy of others. When explaining this point to people, it is helpful to use an analogy.

Imagine that you are speaking with a high-school student who is getting very frustrated with you.

"No," she exclaims," you don't understand! It's *my* body, and I'm allowed to do whatever I want with it!"

"I agree with you that we are allowed to do certain things with our own bodies," you say carefully. "For example, do you agree with me that I have a right to swing my arm?"

"Obviously. You can do whatever you want!"

"Alright. So, I'm swinging my arm, flailing it around

because it's my right to do so. And then my arm swings out and hits you in the face. That's okay, right? Because it's my right to do whatever I want?"

The student rolls her eyes. "That's really dumb! You can't hit me in the face."

"I agree with you. The point I'm trying to make is that I *can't* do whatever I want with my own body. I have the right to bodily autonomy, but so do you. **My rights stop where your rights begin.**"[2]

The idea that our rights are limited because of the rights of others is difficult for many people to accept. Another simple example to illustrate this point is as follows:

"I don't totally see what you're getting at," the student replies. "What do you mean 'my rights stop'?"

"Let me use another example," you answer. "When you're eighteen, you're legally allowed to consume alcohol. At the same time, we know that it's strongly discouraged to drink large amounts because it's not good for you, right?"

"Yeah."

"So if society knows it's not healthy, why do we allow people to do it?"

"I told you before! Because people are allowed to do what they want with their own bodies. We're allowed to make our own decisions."

"I agree with you. However, imagine someone becomes intoxicated. No one stops this person from getting drunk because they figure that person can do whatever she wants.

2   This analogy is presented by Stephanie Gray in *Love Unleashes Life* (Toronto: Life Cycle Books, 2016), 57-58.

But now this person picks up her keys and heads to her car. Is she allowed to get behind the wheel?"

"No, that's super dangerous!"

"Right. But if she's allowed to do whatever she wants with her own body, why would we say she's not allowed to use her body to drive a car?"

"Because if she drives she could hit someone else and kill them," the student answers.

"Exactly," you agree, "because our rights end where the rights of others begin. *We are allowed to do what we want up to a point, but we are not allowed to strip other people of their rights while exercising our own.*"

It is especially important to note that bodily autonomy is not recognized as absolute during pregnancy. In his book *The Case for Life* Scott Klusendorf quotes a thought experiment by Richard Poupard:

> Let's say a woman has intractable nausea and vomiting and insists on taking thalidomide to help her symptoms. After having explained the horrific risks of birth defects that have arisen due to this medication, she still insists on taking it based on the fact that the fetus has no right to her body anyway. After being refused thalidomide from her physician, she acquires some and takes it, resulting in her child developing no arms. Do we believe that she did anything wrong? Would we excuse her actions based on her right to bodily autonomy? The fetus, after all, is an uninvited guest, and has no right even to life let alone an environment free from pathogens.[3]

3   Rich Poupard, "Do No Harm (Except for That Killing Thing)," http://lti-blog.blogspot.com/2007/01/do-no-harm-except-for-that-killing.html, cited in Scott Klusendorf's *the Case for Life.*

By bringing up this thought experiment, Klusendorf emphasizes an important point. We cannot use our bodies to harm others, and this includes during pregnancy. Any physician approached by a pregnant woman requesting thalidomide would have to refuse. This not only proves that there is no such thing as an absolute right to bodily autonomy, but provokes an important question Klusendorf asks those he debates: "So if the mother harms her [pre-]born child with thalidomide that's wrong, but if she kills it with elective abortion that's fine?" It is clear there is a problem with this reasoning, a double standard that pro-choice advocates desperately try to ignore. If the fetus has no rights, a pregnant woman may act as she chooses, and this is a fact that sits uncomfortably with even the staunchest abortion supporters.

4.3 Do the pre-born have a right to another's body?

In emphasizing that our rights end where the rights of another begin, we circle back to the most important question of the abortion debate: **What are the pre-born?** As Randy Alcorn points out, "Once we grant that the [pre-] born are human beings, it should settle the question of their right to live."[4] Once again, the pro-choice movement claims that this is irrelevant. Alcorn quotes Barbara Ehrenreich's 1989 article "The Woman Behind the Fetus," as saying, "A woman may think of her fetus as a person or as just cells depending on whether the pregnancy is wanted or not. This does not reflect moral confusion, but choice in action."[5] The problem here is the same as the problem with the **sentience argument**. Alcorn describes it clearly in this way:

---

4   Randy Alcorn, *ProLife Answers to ProChoice Arguments* (Portland: Multnomah Press, 1992), 77.

5   Barbara Ehrenreich, "The Woman Behind the Fetus," *The New York Times*, April 28, 1989. http://www.nytimes.com/1989/04/28/opinion/the-woman-behind-the-fetus.html.

Testimony Spotlight

"What do you think about abortion?" I asked a high school student walking by.

"I haven't thought about it much before," Logan admitted.

We talked about how all human beings should have human rights, but he wasn't totally convinced.

"But isn't it the woman's body?" he asked. "What about the woman's rights?"

We spoke about how we may not use our bodies to harm others, and how no one has an absolute right to bodily autonomy. After discussing sex-selective abortion and abortion as a form of contraception, Logan said: "Wow, this type of awareness about abortion should be taught in schools! Can I take some extra pamphlets for my Sociology, Anthropology, and Psychology classes?"

I handed him a stack. "Thanks," he exclaimed. "I hope your efforts at educating the public pay off!"

~ Oriyana Hrycyshyn

"One's choice is not made in light of scientific and moral realities. One's choice is itself the only important reality, overshadowing all matters of fact. But if society operated this way, every killing of a person would be justifiable. The real issue would not be the worth of the person killed, but the free choice of the one doing the killing. If a man doesn't want his wife, he can think of her as a nonperson. When he chooses to kill her this is not 'moral confusion' but 'choice in action.'[6]

The difference that pro-choice advocates claim is of ultimate importance, is that the fetus resides within the body of the woman. There is no situation completely analogous to pregnancy. While we may not use our bodies to *harm* others, at the same time we are not required to use our bodies to *sustain* others. One of the most influential arguments in favour of this position was put forward by philosopher Judith Jarvis Thomson.

A. The Violinist Analogy

The crux of Thomson's argument is laid out in Francis Beckwith's *Politically Correct Death: Answering Arguments for Abortion Rights*: "Thomson argues that even if the [pre-]born entity is a person with a right to life, this does not mean that a woman must be forced to use her bodily organs to sustain its life."[7] The analogy Thomson puts forward in her essay is as follows:

> You wake up in the morning and find yourself back to back in bed with an unconscious violinist. A famous unconscious violinist. He has been found to have a fatal kidney ailment, and the Society of Music Lovers has canvassed all the available medical records and found that you alone have the right blood type to help. They have therefore kidnapped you, and last night the violinist's circulatory system was plugged into yours, so that your kidneys can be used to extract poisons from his blood as well as

6   Randy Alcorn, *ProLife Answers to ProChoice Arguments* (Portland: Multnomah Press, 1992), 77-78.

7   Francis J. Beckwith, *Politically Correct Death: Answering Arguments for Abortion Rights* (Grand Rapids: Baker Books, 1993), 128.

your own. The director of the hospital now tells you, "Look, we're sorry the Society of Music Lovers did this to you—we would never have permitted it if we had known. But still, they did it, and the violinist now is plugged into you. To unplug you would be to kill him. But never mind, it's only for nine months. By then he will have recovered from his ailment, and can safely be unplugged from you." Is it morally incumbent on you to accede to this situation? No doubt it would be nice of you if you did, a great kindness. But do you *have* to accede to it?[8]

Obviously, the answer to this question is no; you would not be obligated to remain hooked up to an unconscious violinist. However, as soon as we answer the question this way, pro-choice advocates eagerly pounce, exclaiming, "See? We don't have to use our bodies to sustain someone else! Our bodily autonomy ensures that our bodies cannot be used by anyone against our will." As Klusendorf points out, "There's no mistaking Thomson's claim: Just as one may withhold support and detach himself from the violinist (we are asked to assume), so too the mother may withhold support and detach herself from the child. Abortion is such a detachment."[9]

While at first glance this analogy is troubling, once we take a closer look, we see that there are several problems with this reasoning.

First of all, **responsibility** is of key importance. Scott Klusendorf points out,

"Barring cases of [sexual assault], a woman cannot claim that she bears no responsibility for the pregnancy

8   Judith Jarvis Thomson, "A Defense of Abortion," *Philosophy and Public Affairs 1 (1971), 47-66.* Cited in Francis J. Beckwith, *Politically Correct Death: Answering Arguments for Abortion Rights* (Grand Rapids: Baker Books, 1993), 128.
9   Scott Klusendorf, *the Case for Life* (Wheaton: Crossway Books, 2009), 187.

in the same way that she bears no responsibility to the violinist."[10]

In the vast majority of cases, women become pregnant as a result of consensual sex. When this is the case, a woman and her partner have engaged in an action that is known as fundamentally reproductive. If this act does result in a new life being formed, both parties cannot claim that they were forced into this situation against their will.

In countering this, some may say that while they consented to sex, they did not consent to pregnancy. However, claiming this is claiming that we should not be responsible for the consequences of our actions. Stephanie Gray provides a simple example to illustrate how ludicrous this claim really is: Imagine you are playing baseball with your friends. One of your friends gets a great hit, but the ball soars even farther than it should—right through a neighbour's front window. When you approach your neighbour to explain what happened, you add that you are unwilling to pay for the damage to the window, because while you consented to playing baseball, you did not consent to a window being broken.[11] Obviously, your neighbour would be very unhappy with you.

Ultimately, when we engage in an action we must be willing to accept its logical consequences. Being kidnapped and plugged into a famous violinist is not a logical consequence of going to bed at night. The situation the person in the analogy finds herself in is both unexpected and unnatural. Pregnancy, on the other hand, is neither unexpected nor unnatural. In his article *Unstringing the Violinist*, Greg Koukl explains that the child cannot be regarded as a type of invader, as "a mother's womb is the baby's natural environment . . . One trespasses when he's not in his rightful place, but a baby developing

10   Scott Klusendorf, "Advanced Pro-Life Apologetics," *Biola Document*, 39.
11   Stephanie Gray used this analogy in a training in May of 2014, citing Scott Klusendorf.

in the womb belongs there."[12] Further, as Klusendorf points out, "pregnancy, unlike the violinist analogy, is not a prison bed."[13] It is rare that a pregnancy requires complete bed rest for nine months. Pregnancy tells a woman that her reproductive system is functioning properly, and for many women it is a wonderful experience. Even if it is difficult, we must recognize that actions have consequences. Before we willingly engage in an action, we must first be willing to accept any consequences that could proceed from that action.

"What if, though," someone might counter, "the action was not engaged in willingly? What if the pregnancy came about as a result of sexual assault?" In taking away the **actions have consequences** part of the argument, we must bring forward another point: parents have a responsibility to their offspring that they do not have to strangers. Beckwith quotes Schwarz as saying:

> " . . . the very thing that makes it plausible to say that the person in bed with the violinist has no duty to sustain him; namely, that he is a stranger unnaturally hooked up to him, is precisely what is absent in the case of the mother and her child."[14] As Stephanie Gray has noted, if someone in your city is starving you are not considered responsible, as this person is not one of your dependents. On the other hand, if your children are suffering in your home, you will be charged with neglect.[15] A newborn is entitled to the care of her parents not in spite of her dependence, but because of it. Why

---

12   Greg Koukl, "Unstringing the Violinist," *Stand to Reason,* February 4, 2013. https://www.str.org/articles/unstringing-the-violinist#.WjFJ2iMZO8o.

13   Scott Klusendorf, *the Case for Life* (Wheaton: Crossway Books, 2009), 189.

14   Stephen D. Schwarz, *The Moral Question of Abortion* (Chicago: Loyola University Press, 1990), 118. Cited in Francis J. Beckwith, *Politically Correct Death: Answering Arguments for Abortion Rights* (Grand Rapids: Baker Books, 1993), 131.

15   AbortionNo. "Stephanie Gray at SFLA Conference." YouTube video, 36:00. Posted January 31, 2014. https://www.youtube.com/watch?v=E3YDjFnXHcI&t=760s.

would it be any different with pre-born children? As Beckwith points out, if Thomson claims that parents only become responsible for the children after birth, she is begging the question, as she "cannot appeal to birth as the decisive moment at which parents become responsible in order to prove that birth is the time at which parents become responsible."[16]

In recognizing the duty that parents have to their children it is important to distinguish between *ordinary and extraordinary care*. The Declaration of the Rights of the Child, adopted by the UN General Assembly in 1989, states in Principle 4 that a child

> "shall be entitled to grow and develop in health; to this end, special care and protection shall be provided both to him and to his mother, including adequate pre-natal and post-natal care. The child shall have the right to adequate nutrition, housing, recreation, and medical services."[17]

Essentially, parents have the responsibility to supply their children with the basic necessities of life: adequate nutrition and shelter. This is called **ordinary care.** If a parent fails to provide ordinary care, he/she is held criminally responsible. On the other hand, **extraordinary care** would be providing children with piano lessons, or buying them a pony. While these things may be nice and even valuable to do, they are not required of parents. Because a pre-born child is in the environment in which he/she belongs at that stage of development, and because his/her life can be sustained in no other way, pregnancy can be classified as ordinary care: providing the nutrition and shelter that a child needs to survive.

---

16   Francis J. Beckwith, *Politically Correct Death: Answering Arguments for Abortion Rights* (Grand Rapids: Baker Books, 1993), 131.

17   General Assembly Resolution 1386, "Declaration of the Rights of the Child," *United Nations General Assembly,* accessed December 13, 2017, https://www.unicef.org/malaysia/1959-Declaration-of-the-Rights-of-the-Child.pdf.

B. The Kidney Analogy

The violinist analogy does not hold up under the light of the natural parent-child relationship. However, if the analogy is changed slightly, we are faced with another problem. In a debate with Stephanie Gray, Dr. Andrew Sneddon of the University of Ottawa shifted the analogy to involve a parent-child relationship, arguing that pregnancy is, in fact, extraordinary care on behalf of the mother. His analogy is as follows:

> Suppose that you are in need of a kidney transplant in order to survive and that your mother is the only person in the world who is a physical match, meaning that she is the only person who can provide you with a kidney and hence, preserve your life. Do you have a right to your mother's kidney?[18]

Gray outlined his argument as follows:

> It would be nice for a parent to donate her kidney to her ailing child but the law shouldn't force her [to]. . . In the kidney case, [the child's] right to life and [his/her] need for [his/ her] mother's body to survive do not deliver any right whatsoever to her body, let alone a right that trumps her rights to control her body. The same goes for pregnancy.[19]

A significant difference between this circumstance and abortion is the **cause of death**. This situation cannot be analogous to abortion unless there is something beyond a refusal to donate a kidney: a parent must be allowing their ailing child to be brutally killed. As Beckwith explains, "Euphemistically calling abortion the 'withholding of

18   Stephanie Gray, "A Kidney versus the Uterus," Ethics & Medics, vol. 34, no. 10, October 2009. http://www.ncbcenter.org/em/0910-1.aspx.

19   Stephanie Gray, *Love Unleashes Life* (Toronto: Life Cycle Books, 2016), 57.

support or treatment' makes about as much sense as calling suffocating someone with a pillow the withdrawing of oxygen."[20] The question we need to ask in both situations is: **"How did the child die?"** In the situation of a sick child, the child does not die because you killed her; the child died because she had a kidney ailment. On the other hand, in an abortion, the child died because you directly and intentionally killed her. If nothing is done in the first situation, one person dies, whereas if nothing is done in the second situation, **no one dies.**

What if someone was able to make abortion a simple "unplugging" procedure, rather than a brutal act of killing, similar to the idea of someone being unplugged from the hypothetical violinist? Would this enable pro-choice advocates to claim that abortion is justifiable? If our **points of responsibility for our own actions, ordinary vs. extraordinary care, the importance of a parent-child relationship**, and the **cause of death** are all rejected by an abortion supporter, what are we left with? Since we accede that a mother is not morally obligated to provide her child with her kidney, does that mean that she is not morally obligated to provide her uterus? Stephanie Gray writes:

> While many things could be said in response to the professor's claim, this question needs to be at the heart of our reply: What is the nature and purpose of the kidney versus the nature and purpose of the uterus? The answer tells us why a woman is not obligated to give her child her kidney but is obligated to 'give' her child her uterus.[21]

20 Francis J. Beckwith, *Politically Correct Death: Answering Arguments for Abortion Rights* (Grand Rapids: Baker Books, 1993), 133.

21 Stephanie Gray, "A Kidney Versus the Uterus," *Ethics and Medics,* October 2009, vol 34, no 10. http://d6.endthekilling.ca/sites/default/files/publications/publications_a_kidney_versus_the_uterus.pdf.

Almost every organ in our body, as well as our blood and other tissues, exist in **our** bodies, functioning specifically for the health and well-being of **our** bodies. A woman's uterus is the exception to this. The uterus resides within her body but prepares every month to receive the body of another. The fact that a woman can live without her uterus but her pre-born child cannot shows that the uterus exists more for her pre-born child than it does for her.

4.4 Using Power Responsibly

It is interesting that our society claims that as long as a pre-born child is completely dependent on her mother's body to survive, the mother is able to cherish or dispose of him/her on a whim. In our civilized society, this—excepting the rising assisted suicide rate—is the only situation in which we agree that vulnerability equals disposability. For the most part, we recognize that a heightened dependency on the part of another heightens our responsibility towards that person. This is why we have designated parking spots and ramps alongside stairs for people with disabilities. Accommodations are made for those who are blind or deaf, and we attempt to make our public spaces easily accessible to everyone. We protect and help those who are more vulnerable and dependent than we are. An example I have used in conversation is as follows:

Imagine that you are in a conversation about abortion with a young woman, and she has just said: "But the fetus is completely dependent on the woman's body. Doesn't that mean that the woman can do what she wants with it?"

"I agree with you that the fetus is completely dependent," you say, nodding. "But doesn't someone's dependency on us heighten our responsibility to them, rather than decrease it?"

"What do you mean?"

"Let me use an example. In certain states in the US, the death penalty is legal, but with very strict rules. For example, one of the stipulations to make one eligible for the death penalty is that they must have killed a minor, someone under twelve years of age. Do you think this is because a child is more valuable than an adult?"

"No . . ."

"Then why would this be one of the stipulations?"

"Well, I think if someone kills a kid it's almost worse, not because they're more important, but because they aren't able to defend themselves."

"Right, so they're more dependent on us for protection, right?"

"Yeah."

"So it seems to me, then, that we recognize that when someone is more dependent on us we have *more* responsibility towards them rather than *less*. Who is more dependent than a pre-born child?"

A pre-born child is completely defenseless, entirely vulnerable, and utterly dependent on his/her mother for survival. As a society, we recognize that with great power, comes great responsibility. For example, picture yourself in an airplane, 35,000 feet off the ground. You are in a carefully regulated environment, completely in the power of the pilot. May the pilot decide that he doesn't want you on his plane and order everyone to jump? Or may he decide that he is tired of using his body to direct the flight path of the plane and decide to jump himself, parachuting to safety? Obviously not. The pilot has many people in his care, and he is responsible to get them all to safety.[22]

We would all acknowledge that it would be immoral for the pilot to abandon his passengers, and yet it fits perfectly into the philosophy of bodily autonomy. When people claim that pre-born children are worthy of life once they are no longer fully dependent on their mother's body—the point of viability—they are ignoring the standards our society has set in place regarding how we treat the vulnerable. Alcorn quotes F. LaGard Smith as writing:

> Normally when we see someone mistreated, our sense of outrage, our urge to protect, is inversely related to the person's ability to protect himself: The more *dependent* he or she is, the more protective we become. With "viability" as our guide, we act completely contrary to our normal sense of moral responsibility. Rather than appealing to our best instincts, "viability" brings out the very worst in us.[23]

As Alcorn states, "Too often 'the right to control my life' becomes the right to hurt and oppress others for my own advantage."[24]

A. No other guardian

"Wait," someone might say. "This is all true, *if* there was an option for women to opt out of pregnancy. Of course, parents have a responsibility to their children, but if they want to relinquish this responsibility, they can place their child for adoption. When a woman is pregnant, she doesn't have that option. We can't *force* someone to take care of someone else."

22   Stephanie Gray, *Love Unleashes Life* (Toronto: Life Cycle Books, 2016), 59-60.

23   F. LaGard Smith, *When Choice Becomes God* (Eugene, Ore.: Harvest House, 1990), 146. Cited in Randy Alcorn, *ProLife Answers to ProChoice Arguments* (Portland: Multnomah Press, 1992), 65.

24   Randy Alcorn, *ProLife Answers to ProChoice Arguments* (Portland: Multnomah Press, 1992), 87.

Testimony Spotlight

"I think abortion is mostly wrong," the young woman told me, "but I don't feel that I can tell others what to do. My friend is scheduled to have an abortion next week, and that's her choice."

"Do you believe the pre-born are human beings with human rights?" I asked her.

"Yes, I do. Like I said, I think abortion is wrong, but I'm not going to tell others what to think."

I pointed to my own baby. "Would you take action if I told you I was going to kill him next week?"

"Of course!" she exclaimed. "That would be terrible!"

I pointed to a picture of a first-trimester aborted fetus and asked gently, "Do you think it's any different with your friend's child, who, if you don't do anything, will soon look like that?"

Instantly aware of her responsibility, she asked for pamphlets and contact information for her friend.

~ Maaike Rosendal

At the outset, this statement appears true. Parents may give up both parental rights and responsibilities if they wish to do so, but in the case of pregnancy, the only way to end parental responsibility is by ending the life of the child. The first thing we must do is test the legitimacy of the point that we are not permitted to force someone to care for someone else.

Imagine that on a busy Saturday afternoon you head to your favourite grocery store. As you drive around the parking lot looking for an empty space, you see a car pull out. Quickly, you put your blinker on and pull in, ignoring the annoyed honks of other impatient drivers. As you open your door to leave the vehicle, you notice that you are parked beside a van identical to your own. An hour later, you return to your vehicle, unlocking the doors so that you can load up your trunk. You then turn and return your shopping cart. You breathe a sigh of relief as you climb into the driver's seat and manoeuvre the van out of the parking lot and onto the highway.

You've been driving for about ten minutes when you hear a sneeze come from your back seat. You glance into your review mirror and to your horror, a small child you have never seen before is staring back at you. Immediately you realize what must have happened. The child must have run ahead of his family and gotten into your vehicle, thinking it was his parents' van which was parked right beside yours. This is incredibly inconvenient. You are already 10 minutes away from the grocery store, and you have an urgent appointment to make. The appointment can't be cancelled at this point, and if you're more than fifteen minutes late you will have to pay the full price without getting in, and that is not something you can afford right now.

Well, you think to yourself. *I did not consent to having this child in my back seat. We're not even related, so no one can claim that I have a responsibility to care for him. I don't even like children! I cannot be forced to care for anyone if I don't want to.* With these thoughts in mind, you pull over to the side of the highway, remove the child from your vehicle, and carry on, with plenty of time to make your appointment.[25]

25　This was presented in a CCBR pro-life 201 intern training.

In light of this difficult situation, was this response a legitimate one? Obviously not. When inconvenience, however great, is placed next to the safety of a child, the safety of the child *must* come first. While there was no personal responsibility in creating this situation, and no parental responsibility towards the child, yet it is clear that there was a responsibility to keep the child safe. In this type of situation, Steve Wagner and his colleague Timothy Brahm from Justice for All would have labelled the minivan driver a *de facto guardian*.[26] In order to be a de facto guardian, and have legal responsibilities towards a child, there are three points that Wagner outlines:

1. You are the only person in the immediate geographical vicinity of the child.

2. You are able to help the child.

3. The help the child needs amounts to ordinary care.[27]

Wagner brings forward another example that is more analogous to pregnancy. He writes:

> Imagine that a woman named Mary wakes up in a strange cabin. Having gone to sleep in her suburban home the night before, she starts to scream frantically. She goes to the window and sees snow piled high. It appears she is snowed in. On the desk by the window, she finds a note that says, "You will be here for six weeks. You are safe, and your child is, too. There is plenty of food and water."

Since she just gave birth a week ago, she instinctively begins tearing through each room of the cabin looking for

---

26   Stephen Wagner, "De Facto Guardian and Abortion: A Response to the Strongest Violinist," *Justice for All* (April 13, 2013), 5. http://doc.jfaweb.org/Training/DeFactoGuardian-v03.pdf.

27   Ibid., 4.

her infant son. She finds an infant in a second room, but it is not her infant. It is a girl who appears to be about one week old, just like her son. Mary begins to scream.

Pulling herself together, she goes to the kitchen area of the cabin and finds a huge store of food and a ready source of water. The baby begins to cry, and she rightly assesses that the baby is hungry. Mary sees a three-month supply of formula on the counter in the kitchen area.

Now, imagine that the police show up at the cabin six weeks later, and Mary emerges from the cabin. After determining she is in good health, albeit a good bit frazzled, one policeman says, "We've been investigating this situation for some time. The Behavioural Psychologists from the nearby University of Lake Wobegon are responsible. We'll bring them to justice. We're so glad you're okay. Is there anyone else in the cabin?"

Mary said quietly, "There was."

"There was?" The police hurry past her to the cabin. They search the cabin and find the infant formula unopened on the counter. They find the infant dead on a bed. The coroner confirms that the infant died from starvation.[28]

As Wagner points out, we may have great sympathy for Mary because she was placed in such a difficult position, and yet acknowledge that she did something dreadfully wrong. She had a moral obligation to feed the infant as there was no one else available to do so. Taking this analogy one step further, Wagner removes formula from the equation. Mary is still able to feed the child, as she has recently given birth herself and is lactating. Even though this requires the use

---

28   Stephen Wagner, "De Facto Guardian and Abortion: A Response to the Strongest Violinist," *Justice for All* (April 13, 2013), 5. http://doc.jfaweb.org/Training/DeFactoGuardian-v03.pdf.

of an intimate part of her body, Mary still has an obligation to care for the child as much as she is able. It is clear, then, that not only is it possible that someone is obligated to care for another, but someone may be required to use their own body in order to fulfill another's needs.

Wagner adjusts the analogy to be even more similar to pregnancy this way:

> Consider this adjustment to the Cabin story. Mary must stay in the cabin for 40 weeks before being rescued. The note describes what those 40 weeks will hold and as she progresses through the 40 weeks, sometimes her experience is easier than expected, but for much of the time, it is much more difficult. She has to change the child's diapers and eliminate the child's waste. Sometimes the smell of the child's diapers makes her vomit. Other times, she just feels tired. She develops mastitis, which makes feeding the child painful, but not impossible. In addition, imagine that the child cries continually, and the only way to comfort the child is to carry her around continuously. This, along with gaining weight due to an adverse reaction to breastfeeding, has the effect of making Mary feel like she's carrying around 50 more pounds than normal. The note on the desk also mentions that at the end of 40 weeks, if the child lives, the only way Mary will be able to emerge from the cabin is through 30 hours of difficult work shoveling snow with bare hands while clinging to the child. This snow tunneling will involve her skin and muscles being twisted and strained in incredibly painful ways.[29]

Further, Mary is left a note that informs her that if the

29   Stephen Wagner, "De Facto Guardian and Abortion: A Response to the Strongest Violinist," *Justice for All* (April 13, 2013), 5. http://doc.jfaweb.org/Training/DeFactoGuardian-v03.pdf.

child dies, she will be freed instantly. Even though we can acknowledge that this is an unimaginably difficult situation, yet we would have to say that Mary has both a legal and moral obligation to the child. As Wagner points out:

> "the alternative to her having the burden is that the child dies. In light of this reality, it is difficult to conceive of a way in which the burden could be adjusted to change her obligation to feed the child."[30]

The dependency of another human being heightens our responsibility towards them, even if it places us in difficult situations. That is the reality of living in a just society: rights and responsibility go hand in hand.

4.5 Moral Relativism

While we provide logical answers to pro-choice questions, many pro-choice advocates still believe that they hold the trump card, claiming: "What's right for me is right for me. You can't force your beliefs on me." We are facing what Greg Koukl and Francis J. Beckwith have described as:

> ". . .the extinction of the idea that any particular thing can be known for sure. Today we've lost the confidence that statements of fact can ever be anything more than just opinions; we no longer know that anything is certain beyond our subjective preferences. The word *truth* now means 'true for me' and nothing more."[31]

Essentially, questions of great moral importance have been reduced to preference choices. One may choose to end the

---

30   Stephen Wagner, "De Facto Guardian and Abortion: A Response to the Strongest Violinist," *Justice for All* (April 13, 2013), 5. http://doc.jfaweb.org/Training/DeFactoGuardian-v03.pdf.

31   Francis J. Beckwith and Gregory Koukl. *Relativism: Feet Firmly Planted in Mid-Air.* (Grand Rapids: Baker Books, 1998), 20.

life of their pre-born child in the same way they choose what shirt to wear that day. The famous pro-choice slogan is trotted out tirelessly: "If you don't like abortion, don't have one." "I agree," someone might say, "that abortion is wrong for *you*, so you definitely should not get one. On the other hand, *I* have no problem with it, so it is the right decision for *me*."

This concept is the true meaning behind the slogan *pro-choice*. We are all free to make choices, and we must be tolerant of the choices that others make, even if we disagree with them. Tolerance is the god our Western world worships. It is this principle, as Koukl and Beckwith explain, that is considered "one of the key virtues of relativism. Morals are individual, relativists argue, and therefore we ought to tolerate the viewpoints of others and not pass judgement on their behaviour and attitudes."[32] However, the idea that we must tolerate the views of others is ultimately self-refuting. Klusendorf points out the three major flaws with moral relativism in *The Case for Life*: "First . . . it cannot live by its own rules. Second, relativism cannot reasonably say why anything is wrong . . . Third, it is impossible for anyone to consistently live as a relativist."[33]

All three of these flaws are evident from the moment someone declares: "You can't impose your beliefs on me!" The idea that one should not be permitted to impose their belief on another is itself a belief, and the person espousing it is attempting to impose that belief on others. As Klusendorf outlines, a simple reply can expose this declaration as self-refuting; we need only say, "Why? Why can't I impose my beliefs on you?" Any answer to this question will be an attempt by *them* to impose their beliefs on *you*.[34] In fact, "Relativists inevitably take moral positions just like the rest of us."[35]

---

32   Ibid., 69.
33   Scott Klusendorf, *The Case for Life* (Wheaton: Crossway Books, 2009), 161.
34   Ibid.
35   Ibid., 164.

Relativists preach tolerance until they find someone who disagrees with them. As Beckwith explains:

> "the abortion-rights advocate, by saying that the pro-lifer is obligated not to interfere with the free choice of pregnant women to kill their [pre-]born offspring, is imposing his moral perspective upon the pro-lifer who believes it is her duty to rescue [them]."[36]

The ultimate problem here is that, if morality is simply up to the individual person, there can be no universal guidelines, including the all-important guideline of tolerance.[37]

In claiming that people may do whatever they personally feel is right, pro-choice advocates try to explain why they feel laws protecting pre-born children should not be enacted. However, abortion is one of the only examples of legislating morality that the pro-abortion crowd disagrees with. As Beckwith mentions, we have "laws against drunk driving, murder, smoking crack, robbery, and child molestation," all of which are "intended to impose a particular moral perspective on the free moral agency of others."[38] When we ask those we are having a conversation with about these cases, it is rare that anyone will say that these laws are unjust or even unnecessary.

Once again, we are faced with the only question that really matters in the abortion debate: **are the pre-born human?** Beckwith summarizes the argument this way:

> "A law forbidding abortion would unjustly impose a moral perspective upon another only if the act of

---

36   Francis J. Beckwith, *Politically Correct Death: Answering Arguments for Abortion Rights* (Grand Rapids: Baker Books, 1993), 82.

37   Francis J. Beckwith and Gregory Koukl. *Relativism: Feet Firmly Planted in Mid-Air.* (Grand Rapids: Baker Books, 1998), 69.

38   Ibid., 81-82.

abortion does not limit the free agency of another."[39]

In a civil society, relativism is impossible to live by, as "every right, whether it is the right to life or the right to abortion, imposes some moral perspective on others to either act or not act in a certain way."[40] If pro-choice advocates were truly tolerant, they would tolerate the fact that pro-life advocates feel the need to speak out on behalf of the youngest of their kind. As it appears, they are not very good at living by their own rules.

A. Personally pro-life and morally neutral

While the pro-choice movement may not be good at living by their own rules, some who call themselves pro-life have attempted to conform to them. Those who fall into this category may call themselves one of two things. Either they claim to be "personally pro-life" but feel that they cannot tell others what to do, or they call themselves pro-choice, but, as they will quickly qualify, not because they like abortion. In fact, they would *never* get an abortion themselves, they just want the choice to be open to everyone.

These groups try to present themselves in a position that is entirely neutral, without recognizing that neutrality, in this case, is impossible. Klusendorf writes:

> "Moral neutrality is impossible. Both sides of the abortion controversy bring prior metaphysical commitments to the debate. Why, then, is it okay for liberals to legislate their metaphysical views on the status of the [pre-]born, but not okay for pro-lifers to legislate theirs?"[41]

---

39   Francis J. Beckwith and Gregory Koukl. *Relativism: Feet Firmly Planted in Mid-Air.* (Grand Rapids: Baker Books, 1998), 20.

40   Ibid.

41   Scott Klusendorf, *the Case for Life* (Wheaton: Crossway Books, 2009), 101.

Alcorn reveals the hypocrisy of this idea with an analogy:

> Those who were prochoice about slavery fancied that their moral position was sound since they personally didn't own slaves. Yet it was not just the pro-slavery position, but the prochoice about slavery position, that resulted in the exploitation, beatings, and deaths of innocent people in [the United States].[42]

Those who claim to be "personally pro-life" are, in fact, pro-choice, and those who are pro-choice are essentially the same as those who are pro-abortion. After all:

> "pro-choice people vote the same as pro-abortion people. Both oppose legal protection for the innocent [pre-]born. Both are willing for children to die by abortion and must take responsibility for the killing of those babies even if they do not participate directly."[43]

Claiming that you are against abortion for yourself, but willing to tolerate the choice of others to have an abortion is a completely confused moral stance. When someone claims that they hold this position, we need to ask them: Why? Why do you oppose abortion for yourself? The only valid reason to oppose abortion is if it ends the life of an innocent child. That kind of conversation may look something like this:

"Well," says the young woman, shifting uncomfortably, "I don't like abortion. I would never have an abortion myself. I just don't think we can tell other people what to do."

"Why would you never have an abortion?"

"In my opinion, I think it's totally wrong."

---

42   Randy Alcorn, *ProLife Answers to ProChoice Arguments* (Portland: Multnomah Press, 1992), 102.

43   Ibid.

"Why do you think it's totally wrong? Forgive me, I'm just trying to understand where you're coming from."

"Well, to me abortion is like killing a baby."

"Okay, so just to clarify, you would never kill a baby, but you are okay with other people doing so?"

The above conversation simplifies the issue, revealing what those who are so-called "personally pro-life" are really saying. If we would never say: "I wouldn't personally abuse children, but I don't want to tell others not to," then we can also never claim to be personally pro-life.

4.6 Conclusion

The pleasant word "choice" cloaks a violent, disturbing reality. It can only be established that a woman has a right to choose when we ask the question: the right to choose what? We may have the right to bodily autonomy, but we may never use our rights to infringe upon the rights of others. We have a responsibility to those we have power over, and the more vulnerable they are, the more responsibility we have. When it comes to abortion, we cannot be neutral: either it is wrong, or it is not. Either we have the right to end the life of another human being, or we do not. For those of us who profess to be pro-life, if we truly believe that pre-born children are living human beings, and that abortion violently ends their lives, then it is time that we act like it. However, some reading this may think that it can't possibly be that simple. Things are never completely black and white. There are situations surrounding abortion that cannot be answered in a logical way, and we need to look at these circumstances on a case by case basis. There is no denying that there are situations that seem more complicated, and we address what are called 'the hard cases' in the following section.

Key Takeaways

- The right to bodily autonomy:

    - Exists on a hierarchy of rights. The right to life must be upheld as it is the more fundamental right.

    - Is not absolute. We may not use our bodies to hurt others. Our rights end where the rights of another begin.

- Abortion is not analogous to withdrawal of care or parental kidney donation because of these reasons:

    - **Actions have consequences**. The majority of pregnancies occur when two people make the conscious choice to engage in an act that is fundamentally reproductive.

    - Parents have a **responsibility** towards their children that they do not have towards strangers.

    - Parents must provide their children with **ordinary care**—food and shelter.

    - The **cause of death** in the violinist and kidney analogies is an illness outside of one's control. The cause of death in an abortion is the direct and intentional ending of one's life.

    - The **nature and purpose** of the uterus is to nurture a pre-born child. A woman can live without her uterus; a pre-born child cannot.

Key Takeaways - *continued*

- When there is no alternative guardian, we are responsible for those more vulnerable than we are, *regardless of relation.*

4.7 Diving Deeper

1. We know that we are not permitted to do whatever we like with our own bodies. Are you uncomfortable with the idea that the government can have control in such intimate parts of our lives? Why or why not? How much control is too much? How much is too little?

2. Is there any situation other than pregnancy where someone could have a right to your body?

3. Why is it impossible to be morally neutral? Can you think of situations throughout history where people also tried to make this claim? What happened?

4.8 Suggested Activities

1. Imagine that a new friend has just discovered you are pro-life. "What?" she says, "I don't understand how *you* can tell *me* what to do with *my* body." With a partner, practice responding to this statement.

2. Make a list of the rights you enjoy. What freedoms are the most important? Do your parents or others have rights that you don't? Why?

3. Create a list of positions of power. What is the purpose of these positions? In a small group, discuss what

responsibilities are related to positions of power, and how this power can be abused.

4.9 Additional Resources

- *The Case for Life,* by Scott Klusendorf

    - *The Case for Life* thoroughly addresses the ideas of moral neutrality and the tolerance objection, among many others.

- *Politically Correct Death: Answering Arguments for Abortion Rights,* by Francis Beckwith

    - This book reviews 69 different ethical and philosophical questions surrounding abortion, including the violist analogy.

- *Relativism: Feet Firmly Planted in Mid-Air*, by Francis Beckwith and Gregory Koukl

    - This is a great resource that comprehensively explains the deep philosophical problems with moral relativism, and the ramifications of subscribing to this ideology.

Part Five: The Hard Cases

Is there really no case where abortion is necessary? What about . . .

*"Be kind, for everyone you meet is fighting a battle
you know nothing about."*
Anonymous

5.1 Introduction

"You people really don't understand," a blonde girl exclaimed, storming up to where I stood in front of our pro-life display. "Women *need* abortion!"

"What do you mean by that?" I asked carefully, seeing how upset she was.

"There are situations women are in that are *really* difficult. They need to have abortion as an option."

"I agree with you that there can be extremely difficult circumstances surrounding an unplanned pregnancy," I replied. "However, do we try to alleviate suffering, or do we eliminate people?"

"No!" she snapped, clearly frustrated with my response. "If abortion isn't available, women will *die*!"

"Can you clarify what you mean by that?"

She nodded, calming down when she saw that I was willing to hear what she had to say. "There are medical situations where women will die if they can't terminate the pregnancy. Do you pro-lifers really want a woman to die? What good does that do for the baby? How does it make sense to let both die when you could at least save one?"

"Okay, I see what you're saying. Can you give me a specific example of a medical situation where abortion is necessary to save a woman's life?"

She nodded, tears welling up in her eyes. "Yes, I absolutely can. My aunt was in that situation. She wanted her baby, but she was told that if she didn't have an abortion she was going to die. What was she supposed to do?"

5.2 Is it really that black and white?

Life, many people claim, is too complicated to think in terms of black and white; it is rare that something is simply right or wrong—there are grey areas in every situation. Such a grey area, it is argued, firmly envelops the issue of abortion. For some who label themselves pro-choice, accepting the logical case against abortion is difficult because it seems too simple. The syllogism that we bring forward— human rights are for all human beings, pre-born children are human beings, and therefore, abortion is a human rights violation—is often rejected because it is so straightforward, whereas circumstances rarely are so.

Being pro-life without exception is a radical position to take. For example, many pro-life politicians who unapologetically state that they are against abortion make exceptions for women who have conceived as a result of sexual assault, or when a child has a terminal pre-natal diagnosis, or in a case where the mother's life is in danger. At first glance, it may seem as if these situations hover in a grey area. However, sticking to our syllogism is crucial, for without consistency we have no credibility. As soon as we concede that some situations fall into grey areas, our argument has holes that will fill with the bodies of pre-born children. There are no grey areas, but what we call the **hard cases** are real. These cases are particularly complex and often need to be dealt with differently than the difficult circumstances we discussed in Part One.

A. Sexual Assault

When engaging people in discussion about abortion, it is inevitable that the case of sexual assault will be brought up. The question: *"Well, what about rape?"* is the first question that we need to know how to answer intelligently and compassionately. As pro-lifers, this can be one of the most difficult questions to handle. If we take time to think about how it would feel to become pregnant after being violently assaulted in the most intimate of ways, we can perhaps recognize how abortion may seem like the only way to escape a desperate situation.

When accused of "forcing a woman to have her rapist's baby," we may struggle with how cruel that sounds, and almost feel ashamed of our pro-life views. It may be helpful to remember that according to the same Guttmacher Institute study referenced in Part One, only 1.5% or less of women seeking abortion have become pregnant as a result of rape or incest,[1] while a second study states that the number is only 1%.[2] The rape exception, as it is known, is indeed an exception.

That being said, the fact that this situation is rare makes it no less real, particularly to those who have experienced such trauma. How we deal with this question in discussion may be different, depending on who we are speaking with. First, we need to evaluate why this question came up in a conversation, asking ourselves: *is the person we are speaking with trying to trap us, genuinely interested in our answer, or coming from an emotional place of personal experience, either for themselves or for a loved one?* Our tone and the way we answer the question will be based on this evaluation. Secondly, how we answer this will depend on how much time we have to communicate our position.

1   Lawrence B. Finer, et al., "Reasons U.S. Women Have Abortions: Quantitative and Qualitative Perspectives," *Guttmacher Institute,* September 2005, https://www.guttmacher.org/journals/psrh/2005/reasons-us-women-have-abortions-quantitative-and-qualitative-perspectives.

2   Jane Orient, MD, "The Truth of Forcible Rape, or Public Hysteria," Association of American Physicians and Surgeons; http://www.wnd.com/2012/08/akin-not-far-off-base-in-rape-comment; also referenced, http://www.physiciansforlife.org/content/view/2255/26/.

In a situation where there is minimal time to respond, we do not always have time to completely go through common ground, analogy, and question, and we may have to skip the analogy. It is important to find common ground when talking about *any* difficult circumstances, but in this case it is particularly important to show that we have the same abhorrence of sexual assault as the people we are speaking with. We can do this by saying something like: "I agree with you, sexual assault is horrible, and rapists should get tracked down and prosecuted to the full extent of the law." After stating this quietly and firmly, we should pause for a moment to let it sink in before continuing to a crucial question: **"Is it fair, though, in a country that does not give the death penalty to the guilty rapist, to give the death penalty to the innocent child?"**[3] The purpose of this question is not to advocate for the death penalty, but to use an analogy that immediately conveys the injustice of abortion as the proposed solution, even in this difficult situation. For many people, their focus is on the unimaginable pain that the woman is suffering, and seething with righteous anger, they want justice to be executed. Our task is to show them that their anger is misdirected. Justice must be done, but the one who must be punished is the guilty rapist, rather than the innocent child whose life was created as a result of his brutal crime.

There is another question we can ask when we have minimal time to get our point across, particularly when someone is against all abortion except in the case of sexual assault. "What if I told you," we may say, "that one of the people we can see right now was conceived in rape. Would you be able to tell me which one?" The answer to this question, obviously, is no. We can't tell the circumstances in which a human being was conceived by looking at them.

---

3   A variation of this question was presented on the CCBR's previous online pro-life classroom.

When we look at another person, what we see is a human being, and that human being has infinite value, regardless of how he or she was conceived.

In conversations where we have a bit more time, we may choose to **trot out the toddler.**

As the practices in Part One illustrate, such a conversation could go something like this:

"I agree with most of what you're saying, but what if someone is raped?"

"Sexual assault is horrible," you begin, finding **common ground**. "I can't imagine what it would be like to experience that kind of trauma, or how I would feel if I got pregnant as a result of being attacked." Then you continue with an **analogy**: "Imagine this. A woman is raped a day after having sex with her husband. When she discovers that she is pregnant, she is uncertain who the child's father is. She decides to carry through with the pregnancy, and after the child is born she has a paternity test taken. The test reveals that the father of the baby is not her husband, but the rapist, and she is so overcome with horror that she drives to a bridge and throws her baby into the water. Do you think that what she did was okay?"[4]

"Of course not! That's awful!"

"I agree. If she shouldn't be allowed to kill her born child because of rape, then why should she be permitted to kill her pre-born child because of that same situation?"

The circumstance brought forward in this mock conversation is not completely fabricated. The *New York Times* published an article called "Telling the Stories Behind the Abortions," in which Cornelia Dean relates the

4   This analogy was first presented in CCBR's previous pro-life classroom.

experience of one abortionist:

> Dr. Wicklund describes her horror when she aborted the pregnancy of a woman who had been raped, only to discover, by examining the removed tissue, that the pregnancy was further along than she or the woman had thought—and that she had destroyed an embryo the woman and her husband had conceived together.

Dr. Wicklund was horrified because she destroyed what would have been a wanted child, created through an act of love.[5] **However, how we feel about a child does not change what he or she is: a human being.** Our feelings do not dictate who is valuable and who is not: our humanity does.

At times, the person with whom we are speaking may become very emotional. In these cases, it is possible that a loved one experienced sexual assault and made the decision to have an abortion. They may even confide in you that this has happened to them personally. We need to be very careful with how we speak to such people, and the importance of empathy cannot be overemphasized. At times this means that we drop the topic of abortion altogether and focus on the needs of the person in front of us. It is important that we ask questions such as: **"Is the person who hurt you still in your life?"** and **"Do you have people in your life that you have told and that are helping you with this?"** We need to offer them the help they need. It is possible that this information has never been disclosed before. In conversations where personal experiences are shared, people are usually not wondering if *pre-born children* are human beings, they are wondering if *we* are, based on whether we can empathize with fellow human beings in tragic circumstances.

Discussing sexual assault is not easy, because when we put ourselves in the shoes of a woman pregnant after

---

5   This story was presented on CCBR's online pro-life classroom.

being attacked, we can see how, blinded by inconceivable pain and terror, abortion would appear to be the best way out of the situation. What we need to remember is that it only seems as if it is the best way to escape further pain. Ultimately, compounding an injustice does not provide retribution. One victim has suffered immeasurably, and abortion will not take away that trauma. While her right to choose was brutally torn from her, does the solution include allowing her living, growing child to be brutally torn from her womb? There is no easy answer to this question, because it is not an easy situation. There are no words powerful enough to condemn the crimes of the rapist, there are no words adequate to describe the pain that a woman who has been violated suffers, and there are no words sufficient to convey the urgency of the situation for these precious pre-born children. However, we must try, for the alternative is truly unthinkable: rapists unpunished, women unaided, and countless innocent children in the trash.

B. Pregnant Minors

In 2015, the Western world was shaken by reports that an 11-year-old in Paraguay, South America, was pregnant as a result of sexual assault. In Paraguay, abortion is illegal except in cases where the life of the mother is at risk. Pro-choice advocates at once began clamoring at the injustice of this child being denied an abortion. The UN published a report in 2013 estimating that 2 million girls under the age of 14 give birth in underdeveloped countries every year.[6] It is undeniable that these cases entail the most brutal circumstances an unplanned pregnancy can consist of. The question is often posed in this way: "Do you honestly want a *child* to give birth? You would force a *child* to do that?" The

---

6   Rafael Romo & Sanie López Garelli, "11-year-old rape victim denied abortion gives birth in Paraguay," CNN.com, August 14, 2015, http://www.cnn.com/2015/08/13/americas/paraguay-young-rape-victim-gives-birth/index.html.

Testimony Spotlight

"Hello, sir, what do you think about abortion?" I asked a man walking by.

"I'm against it," he replied, "except in situations where a woman has been raped."

"I couldn't imagine what a woman goes through when she's in that kind of situation," I said, finding common ground. "Talking about sexual assault is one of the most difficult situations to deal with. Our priority needs to be to help the victim of sexual assault and bring the perpetrator to justice."

"I couldn't agree more!" He nodded for emphasis.

I carried on by trotting out the toddler: "Imagine, though, that a woman in such a situation decides to carry the child to term and has a little boy. A year later, this child begins to remind her of the rapist, something unimaginably difficult. Would it be okay for her to kill that one-year old?"

He thought for a moment before a look of understanding crept across his face. "Wow, you got me. Yeah, that makes sense! I've never thought of it like that."

To reinforce that point, I asked a question. "If we don't even have the death penalty for the guilty rapist, why should we have it for the innocent child?"

"Right, that totally makes no sense," he exclaimed.

Testimony Spotlight - *continued*

"I can't believe that I just said that abortion would be okay!" As he turned to leave he said, "Thank you very much," and reached out to shake my hand.

~Alex Vande Bruinhorst

answer, obviously, is one-thousand times **no.** Our hearts break for the children forced into these immeasurably traumatic situations. No one wants a child to be a mother. Even more importantly, no one wants her to be raped in the first place. In these cases, people often focus on the wrong point: the injustice is not that she is pregnant, the injustice is that she was impregnated. The person who sexually assaulted a child is the one who forced her into these traumatic circumstances, and this trauma will not be undone by having an abortion. In fact, very few women choose abortion after having been raped. What is significant to note in this particular case, and nearly every case like it, is that the girl herself is never referenced as having requested abortion; rather, her mother did.

While the world is declaring that what she and all girls facing similar circumstances need is abortion, what we should be focused on is not a band-aid solution. We ought to be seeking help for these girls and attempting to ensure that they are not in dangerous situations to begin with. However, prevention is never 100% effective and injustices will always occur. The question is: are we going to address or add to injustice? If people, sometimes even pro-lifers, are leaning toward allowing abortion in such circumstances, they have lost sight of the fact that there are two children in question.

One human being was brutally violated, and another human being was conceived as a result of this violence. Both persons are innocent; both persons are deserving of all the rights, protection, and help that we can afford them. This is not to say that there are not serious health risks that pregnancy can pose for mothers who are extremely young. Addressing these risks is imperative and must be taken on a case by case basis. How to address medical emergencies will be discussed later in this chapter.

C. Terminal Pre-natal Diagnosis

The topic of terminal pre-natal diagnoses is not as common as the sexual assault exception, but it can also be emotional. When people refer to terminal pre-natal diagnoses, the question is often asked this way: *"What if the baby is just going to die anyway?"* In these cases, a pre-born child has been medically termed **incompatible with life.** This means that they will probably not live until birth, and if they do, they will likely pass away within hours of being born. The phrase *incompatible with life* is one that every parent dreads to hear, and it is a crippling emotional blow.

It is important to note that in the majority of these cases, the parents want and love their child. They did not come to their doctor's appointment seeking an abortion. Once they are informed that their child is not the healthy child they hoped for, and that he/she will very likely pass away in the near future, they understandably begin to search for a way to deal with this devastating news. Sadly, abortion is often promoted to these grieving parents as a way to cope. After all, the reasoning goes, the child is going to die anyway. Why would one wait with the terrible uncertainty that each day may be their child's last? Why go through the trauma of birth, only to lose your child during labour or in the moments afterward? Isn't it better to just let go now, to say your good-byes as soon as possible and move on with your life?

Clarifying Terms

Trisomy

In cases of a poor or terminal pre-natal diagnosis, a child is often diagnosed with a form of trisomy other than Down Syndrome, such as Edwards Syndrome, also known as Trisomy 18, or Trisomy 13 (Patau Syndrome). These conditions are a consequence of faulty cellular division that occurs early in pregnancy, resulting in additional genetic information. Children with these conditions are often severely disabled and have multiple problems with different organs, particularly their lungs and heart. Different forms of trisomy, such as Trisomy 15 or Trisomy 21 result in early miscarriage. However, it is a myth that the diagnosis of Trisomy is always terminal. People with some forms of Trisomy can actually survive and live for quite some time if they have reparative heart surgery after birth (https://www.youtube.com/watch?v=bzPK4Kjtxuk).

Ultimately, what this reasoning is attempting to do is restore control. As human beings, one of the most difficult things to accept is that we do not have absolute mastery over our lives. When a couple is told that their child cannot survive, they are faced with a situation in which they have no power over succeeding events. The fact that a loved one will soon pass away is extremely difficult to deal with. Abortion offers a semblance of control, where the choice of when a child's final moments will be is left to the parents. They have entered a nightmare, and abortion is being offered as a way to wake them up.

Once again, abortion appears to be the solution, a cure-all in a situation in which there is no real cure. A child exists, and that life is not something that can be erased from memory. The situation is tragic and there is no way to escape it: The only thing left is how the parents choose to respond to the situation. In conversation with people, there is a simple **analogy** that can be very helpful:

Imagine you have just asked a young man what he thinks about abortion, and he responds with: *"I think it should be allowed if the baby is going to die anyway."*

"I agree with you," you reply, "that such a situation is tragic. I can't imagine what it would feel like to have to deal with something like that. I just have one question for you. If someone you love, who lived far away, was diagnosed with cancer and was given three weeks to live, would you wait until day twenty to go visit him or her? Or would you leave right away to spend every precious moment that you could with this person?"

"I'd leave right away, of course!"

"Me too! It seems to me, then, that we agree that when someone we love has only a short time left to live, that we don't minimize the time we have. Rather, we try to treasure the time that we have left—wouldn't you say?"

"Yeah, I would say that."

"Wouldn't it make sense, then, that someone who is told their child has only a short time left to live, would not cut it short, but treasure every last moment that they have with their child?"

"Okay, I guess that makes sense. But it would be really hard!"

Testimony Spotlight

"Hello," I greeted a young couple walking by. "What do you think about abortion?"

"I don't really know," the young man replied, and his girlfriend nodded in agreement.

I went through **the human rights argument** with them, and they agreed that since a pre-born child is a living human being, and we believe in human rights, abortion must be a human rights violation. I followed up with: "Can you think of any situation where abortion should be allowed?"

"No!" the girl responded firmly.

The young man was a bit more unsure. "I had a sister who was born with many health difficulties," he told me. "She was only given eleven years to live, but she lived just over twice that long. But she suffered a lot. Sometimes I wonder if it wouldn't be better just to stop their suffering before they're even born."

"That must have been very difficult for your family," I told him, "and I agree with you that it's awful how some people have to suffer. However, do we really know if someone else's life is worth living?"

"No, I guess not," he replied.

"What do you think would be better," I asked, **"to try our best to alleviate suffering, or just eliminate sufferers?"**

Testimony Spotlight - *continued*

"When you put it that way, abortion definitely makes no sense!" He agreed, and he and his girlfriend walked away 100% pro-life.

~ Brittany Van de Bruinhorst

"I agree with you, it *would* be incredibly hard. **But what would be harder, do you think: knowing that you loved and cherished your child for every moment that they were in your life, or knowing that you had the life of your child ended?**"[7]

The final question of this illustration really sums up what we want to say. No one is denying that being told your loved one will likely never make it to birth is tragic. No one is trying to minimize what these parents are going through. The truth we are trying to communicate is that there is no way to erase a child that already exists. No matter what happens, a very real loss will be experienced. The question is this: Will the pre-born child be treated with the love and respect that he or she deserves? Will their life, however short, be cherished, or will it be brutally cut short? There is no solution to this kind of situation, but abortion is neither an easy response nor a moral one.

5.3 The Life of the Mother

The question whether abortion is moral when the mother's life is in danger is often the exception that even stalwart pro-lifers concede to. Initially, it seems logical; at a

---

7   This analogy was presented in Stephanie Gray's *Love Unleashes Life* (Toronto: Life Cycle Books, 2016), 96-97.

certain stage, if the mother dies, her pre-born child dies. It makes no sense to allow two people to die when we have the opportunity to save at least one. However, abortion is not merely allowing someone to die, but it is the active facilitator in the death of a pre-born child. Since we already know that ending the life of an innocent human being is never justifiable, we seem to have run into a serious problem. We know that we cannot kill an innocent human being in order to save another, and yet if the situation remains unchanged, both mother and child will die. For example, if a close friend has a heart condition, we may not kill a stranger, remove the stranger's healthy heart, and use it to save our friend's life. Though a good result was achieved—our friend's life was saved—it was achieved through an immoral act, and the ends do not justify the means. We cannot kill to save.

This does not mean that we can do nothing. First, it is important to note that a situation in pregnancy where a woman's life is threatened is rare, making up less than 1% of abortions. Secondly, **abortion is never necessary to save the life of the mother.** This statement requires explanation: Dr. C. Everett Koop, who served as an United States Surgeon General, stated that in his thirty-eight years as a pediatric surgeon "he was never aware of a single situation in which a pre-born child's life had to be taken in order to save the life of the mother."[8] Further, the **Dublin Declaration on Maternal Healthcare** states:

> "As experienced practitioners and researchers in obstetrics and gynaecology, we affirm that direct abortion—the purposeful destruction of the [pre-] born child—is not medically necessary to save the life of a woman."[9]

---

8   Randy Alcorn, *ProLife Answers to ProChoice Arguments* (Portland: Multnomah Press, 1992), 167.
9   Committee for Excellence in Maternal Healthcare, "Dublin Declaration on Maternal Healthcare," 2012, https://www.dublindeclaration.com.

Clarifying Terms

Life vs. Health

It is important to clarify whether we are speaking about a woman's *life* or a woman's *health*. When referring to the necessity of abortion due to the life and health of the mother, health has proven to be a subjective term, including not just physical and mental health, but social and even economic health as well. When a pregnancy is adversely affecting a woman's *health*, it does not necessarily mean that it is endangering her *life*. For example, there are pregnancy complications where in order to preserve the life of her child, a woman must go on bed rest for the duration of her pregnancy. This is undeniably a difficult situation. However, it is perfectly reasonable to expect a woman to endure these difficulties, as the only alternative is a dead child.

This declaration has, to date, been signed by over 1013 medical professionals, including obstetricians/ gynecologists, midwives, and neonatologists.

The important distinction here can be found in the words **direct abortion.** In the medical community, the word abortion does not necessarily refer to the direct and intentional killing of a pre-born child. The National Center for Health Statistics defines abortion as occurring when "a fetus or embryo [is] removed or expelled from the uterus during the first half of gestation—20 weeks or less,"[10] which means that "the

---

10   FG Cunningham, et al. (2010). "1. Overview of Obstetrics". *Williams Obstetrics* (23 ed.). McGraw-Hill Medical. ISBN 978-0-07-149701-5.

standard medical definition of abortion [is the] termination of a pregnancy when the fetus is not viable."[11] A miscarriage is often called a "spontaneous abortion." In other words, it is important to be aware that certain ethical life-saving procedures—such as early induction of labour or emergency caesareans, which will be discussed later in more depth—may still be called abortions by the medical community. As pro-lifers, our issue lies with procedures that directly target the body of the pre-born child in an act of violence.

A. The Principle of Double Effect

To illustrate that direct abortion is never necessary, an important question is outlined by Stephanie Gray in *Love Unleashes Life*: **"What medical condition in the *woman's* body will be fixed by us attacking the *baby's* body?"**[12] Rarely is a medical issue completely solved through direct abortion; additional medical treatment is nearly always necessary. In order to understand what medical treatment is ethical, we must apply what is called the **Principle of Double Effect**, summarized by Thomas Cavanaugh in the following way:

> Performing an act with two morally significant effects is justified if:
>
> 1. *the evil effect is not intended as a means or an end, and*
>
> 2. *there is a proportionately serious reason for allowing the evil effect.*[13]

To explain these conditions, we can look at one of the

---

11   George J. Annas, Sherman Elias (2007). "51. Legal and Ethical Issues in Obstetric Practice". In Gabbe, Steven G.; Niebyl, Jennifer R.; Simpson, Joe Leigh. *Obstetrics: Normal and Problem Pregnancies* (5 ed.). Churchill Livingstone. ISBN 978-0-443-06930-7.

12   Stephanie Gray, *Love Unleashes Life* (Toronto: Life Cycle Books, 2016), 63.

13   Cavanaugh, Thomas. "The Intended/Foreseen Distinction's Ethical Relevance." *Philosophical Papers* 25, no. 3 (1996): 179-88.

more common medical situations that can occur during pregnancy, a tubal ectopic pregnancy. In a tubal ectopic pregnancy, the newly formed embryo remains in the fallopian tube and implants there, rather than implanting in the uterus. As the embryo grows and develops, the tube expands. Long before the pre-born child reaches the age of viability, the tube will rupture, resulting in the death of the child and possibly that of the mother as well. In such a medical situation intervention is necessary.

There are two procedures that could be performed: a *salpingotomy* or a *salpingectomy*. In a *salpingotomy*, the fallopian tube is opened, and the embryo is scraped out. If we hold this procedure up to the **principles of double effect**, we find that it fails.[14] The action itself is not a good action, as it is a direct abortion. The good effect, the mother's life being saved, occurs *as a result of* her child dying. In other words, the abortion is the *means* of saving the mother's life. If technology develops to the point where we would be able to save the child through use of an incubator or artificial womb, a salpingotomy would not allow for the child to be saved, as the life of the mother is dependent on the child's body being dismembered. Therefore, a salpingotomy cannot be found ethical.

A salpingectomy, on the other hand, is a procedure in which the medical problem is directly addressed, and the swollen fallopian tube is removed. As a side effect of this procedure, the developing embryo dies. However, the embryo does not pass away because we directly targeted his or her body but dies because we were unable to save his/her life. This procedure is a morally good or neutral act. The good effect comes as a result of the tube being removed, the death of the child was **not intended**, just tolerated, and finally, the saved life of the mother is equal to the bad effect: the death

---

14   A salpingotomy would not be considered unethical if the embryo has already passed away, only if the embryo is still living when the procedure is performed.

of her child. Further, if technology was developed that would enable us to save the lives of these very young children, a salpingectomy would provide that opportunity, allowing us to simply transfer the child to safety. We can conclude, then, that a salpingectomy is an ethical procedure.[15] As a side note, many people question the salpingectomy procedure as they worry it will reduce their fertility. Ultimately, the salpingectomy would still be the only ethical option in this situation even if it did reduce fertility, but evidence shows that in most cases, women with one ovary are able to become pregnant as easily as women with two.

B. The Drowning Analogy

When addressing this question in conversation, many people wonder: what is the difference? No matter which procedure is performed, the result is the same: a child has died. However, we can agree that intent matters. The following **analogy** is often helpful in conversation:

> Imagine that you see two people struggling to swim in a river. You can only save one at a time, so you dive into the water, swim to the middle of the river, and pull the person closest to you to shore. By the time you turn around, the other person has sunk under the water and disappeared. Are you guilty of the death of that person? Of course not!

> In a second situation, you swim out and grab the person closest to you, and then you push the other person's head under water until they have drowned. Now are you guilty of the death of that person? Yes, you are.[16]

---

15 There is debate within the pro-life community regarding these procedures. We decided to keep this example in this resource in order to illustrate the principle of double effect, noting that research and discussion is ongoing.

16 Stephanie Gray, *Love Unleashes Life* (Toronto: Life Cycle Books, 2016), 66.

This analogy illustrates that though the result is the same—one person has drowned— that result came about very differently. In the second case, a person died because you **directly and intentionally killed** that person, whereas in the first situation, a person died because you were **unable to save them**. In the same way, we are never permitted to directly target the body of a pre-born child in order to end their life, but we *are* permitted to target a medical problem. In these cases, a child dies not as a direct result of our intervention, but because we were unable to save them.

In more complicated medical cases, such as HELLP syndrome or pre-eclampsia, there are times when, to save the life of the mother, a pregnancy must be ended. In these cases, the ethical response is not abortion, but rather early induction of labour or an emergency c-section. Both actions would result in the death of the child if he/she is not yet at the age of viability outside the womb. However, the child passes away as a result of a current lack of life-saving technology at such a young age, not because he or she was torn apart through abortion. It is also important to know that the majority of these medical emergencies arise when a woman is over twenty-four weeks pregnant, which means that the child has a fighting chance of survival. Even when a child tragically does not survive these circumstances, he or she was still treated with the dignity and respect they deserve.

C. Real Life Hard Case Example: Savita Halappanavar

In 2012, the debate in Ireland over legalized abortion exploded with the tragic deaths of Savita Halappanavar and her pre-born daughter Prasa. Media outlets around the world were quick to point out that Halappanavar was denied the abortion that could have addressed her condition—septicemia, or a blood stream infection—and saved her life. The case is often presented as a clear example of the necessity of abortion to save a mother's life. However, what

Testimony Spotlight

I engaged a woman in front of our display on the issue of abortion.

"I'm totally against abortion," she told me.

"Do you think there are any situations where abortion is acceptable?" I asked.

She thought for a moment. "Well, if the life of the mother is in danger because of the pregnancy, I think she needs to be able to access abortion."

"There definitely are dangerous medical situations that need to be addressed during pregnancy," I agreed, "but did you know that medical experts worldwide have agreed that abortions are never medically necessary? **The Dublin Declaration** is signed by over 1000 medical professionals, and it states that we never need to target the pre-born child to save the mother's life."

"I didn't know that," she replied. "I like that new perspective."

In order to explain further, I used **the illustration of trying to save two drowning humans** but being unable to save one. This analogy helped her to understand what I was trying to say, and she was encouraged in her new position. We introduced ourselves to each other and she gave me her contact information so that she could become more involved in pro-life efforts.

~ Jeremy Hooghiem

many news reports failed to discuss was that an autopsy revealed that in addition to septicemia, Halappanavar had E.coli ESBL, an antibiotic-resistant bacteria that is associated with urinary tract infections.

The fact that E.coli ESBL was present is significant, as this type of bacteria can lead to septicemia. In fact, *The Journal of Antimicrobial Chemotherapy* records that E.coli is one of the most common organisms to cause urinary tract infections (UTIs), and complicated UTIs are often associated with pregnancy. This information means that it is difficult to reach a definite answer as to how Halappanavar actually died, and it calls into question how ending the life of baby Prasa through abortion would have killed the E.coli.

It is possible that the E.coli ESBL was present in Halappanavar's uterus, as a result of ascending into her vagina and entering via the dilated cervix. In this case, in order to save her life, the infected membranes would have had to be eliminated from her uterus. The ethical course of action in this situation would have been to induce labor, which would have targeted her condition—expelling the infected membranes—rather than directly ending the life of her pre-born daughter through an abortion.

However, it is also possible that the E.coli ESBL ascended her urinary tract and caused an infection in her kidneys. This type of infection can lead to uterine contractions that, left untreated, can result in cervical change. If this was the case, induction of labour would not have eliminated the E.coli ESBL, and because this bacteria is resistant to antibiotics, this is what could have led to septicemia.[17]

What many news reports did not mention regarding this case is that medical inquest revealed a string of

---

17   Much of this information was presented in an article by Stephanie Gray entitled, "Legal Abortion Not the Answer In Ireland Deaths," published on CCBR's blog.

preventable human errors which resulted in the necessary medical action not being taken. For example, while a blood test was taken when Halappanavar first arrived at the hospital which showed an elevated white blood cell count, this information was not recorded on her chart. Further, her vitals were not checked every four hours, and several clear signs of sepsis were missed.[18] These discoveries were found in the investigative reports by the Health Information and Quality Authority and the Health Service Executive, as well as the Coroner's Court inquest into Halappanavar's death.[19]

Ultimately, what can be learned from this tragic story is that it is possible that an ethical course of action was necessary, but in neither case was abortion the answer. When the media used this story to further the case for legalized abortion in Ireland, they forgot a fundamental moral principle: **we may not kill to save.**

5.4 Other Objections

A. Do Abortion Restrictions Really Make a Difference?

In venturing into so-called grey areas, people often want to point out that in some cases, abortion is choosing the lesser of two evils. After all, the claim goes, abortion restrictions do not actually reduce the number of abortions. All abortion restrictions do is force women to get illegal, unsafe, coat-hanger abortions, causing hundreds of thousands of women to die. **Both claims are objectively false.**

The idea that abortion restrictions do not reduce the number of abortions is based primarily on a study published in the prestigious medical journal *The Lancet,*

18   Life Institute. "The facts about the tragic death of Savita Halappanavar." https://thelifeinstitute.net/info/the-tragic-death-of-savita#.
19   Ibid.

called "Induced abortion: incidents and trends worldwide from 1995 to 2008."[20] This study apparently proves that liberal abortion laws *do* result in abortion being safe, legal, and rare. However, there are several severe problems with the findings that supposedly prove the ineffectiveness of restrictive abortion laws.

The main problem with *The Lancet* study, as Ross Douthat of the *New York Times* points out, is that it does not compare like to like.[21] The study looks at the Western world, mainly North America and Western Europe, and compares these abortion rates to those of regions in Southeast Asia and Sub-Saharan Africa. The number of potential confounding variables when comparing rich regions with far poorer regions is staggering. Canada and the United States are hardly analogous to Sub-Saharan Africa. In order to really discern the effect of restrictive abortion laws in North America, we should compare countries that are part of the developed world.

When we do compare regions in developed countries, the result we receive is quite different. In another article responding to *The Lancet* study, political science professor Dr. Michael New points out that America's red states—Republican—have more pro-life laws and lower abortion rates than blue states—Democrat. For example, Massachusetts is known as a Democratic stronghold, and the only restriction on abortion is that a minor must have parental consent. In Mississippi, one of the most Republican states in the US, there are counselling requirements, waiting periods, parental consent laws, ultrasound requirements,

20   Gilda Sedgh, et al., "Induced abortion: incidence and trends worldwide from 1995-2008," *The Lancet* 379, no. 9816 (2012): 625-632, doi: http://dx.doi. org/10.1016/S0140-6736(11)61786-8.
21   Ross Douthat, "What Reduces Abortion Rates," *The New York Times* (February 21, 2012), https://mobile.nytimes.com/blogs/douthat/2012/02/21/ what-reduces-abortion-rates/?referrer=.

and Medicaid coverage only in specific cases. According to the study, Massachusetts should have lower abortion rates, but the opposite is the case.[22] In Europe, Catholic-influenced countries such as France, Italy, Spain, and Germany have more restrictive abortion laws and lower abortion rates than Scandinavian nations. Douthat also mentions Ireland, where up until recently abortion was illegal except in cases where the life of the mother is at risk. As of 2018, Ireland's abortion rate was about one quarter of the abortion rate in England, which has very liberal abortion laws.

Further studies, such as a study conducted by MH Medoff of California State University's Department of Economics called "The Impact of State Abortion Policies on Teen Pregnancy Rates," show that restrictive abortion laws do have an impact on abortion rates. The price of abortion, as well as waiting period laws, have an effect particularly on unmarried women. These laws, he says, "induce unmarried women to change their level of unprotected sexual activity or contraceptive behaviour, thereby reducing the likelihood of an unwanted non-marital pregnancy."[23] Additionally, as abortion availability provides insurance against unwanted birth, restrictive abortion laws, which also increase the cost of obtaining an abortion, increase the incentive to avoid pregnancy. "Pregnancy avoidance behaviour," as Medoff calls it, results in fewer unwanted pregnancies. Empirical results from the studies cited in his research that look at how policy restrictions affect teen pregnancy show that Medicaid funding restrictions and informed consent laws result in fewer unwanted teen pregnancies.

Restrictive abortion laws *do* make a difference on the

---

22   Dr. Michael New, "Pro-Life Laws Are Successful in Reducing Abortion Rates," LifeNews.com, March 5, 2012, http://www.lifenews.com/2012/03/05/pro-life-laws-are-successful-in-reducing-abortion-rates/.

23   Marshall Medoff, "The Impact of State Abortion Policies on Teen Pregnancy Rates," *Social Indicators Resarch* 97 (2010): 177-189, doi: 10.1007/s11205-009-9495-9.

number of abortions. The logic is simple, going back to psychological theories of reinforcement and punishment. If we want something to happen, we reinforce the action; when we don't, we apply restrictions. It may be true that abortion laws will not *end* abortion, in the same way that laws against sexual assault have not been successful in completely eradicating sexual assault from our society. However, we can see throughout the developed world that abortion laws result in fewer abortions. Besides, this claim is merely side-stepping the issue. Even if abortion laws made very little difference, and even if the difference could be called statistically insignificant, every human life is worthy of protection.

B. Illegal, Unsafe Abortion

In addition to the claim that abortion restrictions do nothing to change the abortion rate, abortion advocates state that restrictions force women underground to seek illegal, unsafe abortions, resulting in a higher rate of maternal death. Legal abortion, they assert, saves lives. This assertion has often been touted by pro-choice activists as a completely factual claim. However, when the facts themselves are brought to the table, they are not exactly what they are said to be.

It is important to note that accurate numbers are extremely difficult to come by. How, exactly, do we keep track of a procedure that is illegal? Former abortionist Dr. Bernard Nathanson confessed in his book *Aborting America*, that, while advocating for abortion, he and his associates at the National Abortion Rights Action League fabricated both the number of illegal abortions performed before Roe vs. Wade and the amount of deaths occurring as a result of these abortions. They claimed that one million women received illegal abortions per year, while a more accurate number could be estimated at about one tenth of that, approximately ninety-eight thousand abortions per year. Further, Nathanson and his colleagues claimed that five to ten thousand women died from these illegal abortions every year.[24] However, research confirms that this number is also a fabrication, as Nathanson outlines in his book. Before abortion was legalized in the United States, the number of women dying from illegal abortions averaged at about two hundred and fifty a year.[25]

From this information, we can establish two points. First, the numbers that abortion advocates present us with are blown up in order to make "safe" abortion appear to be the more compassionate option. These claims can be refuted not only by pointing out the inaccuracy of the numbers, but by clarifying the words *safe abortion*. There is no such thing as a safe abortion, as every abortion violently ends the life of an innocent human being. Abortion is *never* safe for pre-born children, and therefore cannot be labelled a safe procedure.

The second point we need to take note of is that women do die from unsafe abortions. Though the number is far smaller than abortion advocates would have us believe, these deaths do happen. Desperate women in desperate circumstances seek abortion, and these women need compassion and help. However, a procedure becoming unsafe does not automatically necessitate making it legal. For example, some people steal from cars by breaking one of the vehicle's windows and reaching in to unlock the door. In some cases, these people have cut themselves on the broken glass. As a society, we would agree that giving these thieves protective gloves would not be a reasonable solution to this crisis. Essentially, the answer to maternal mortality is not to help mothers do away with their children, but rather to provide them with the adequate health care and resources to deal with their situation.

---

24   Bernard Nathanson, *Aborting America* (New York: Doubleday, 1979), 193.

25   Ibid., 42.

Setting the Record Straight

Maternal Mortality

The claim that maternal mortality rates increase as a result of illegal abortion is completely false. Until recently, Ireland has had heavy restrictions on abortion and has some of the lowest maternal mortality rates in the world. South Africa's maternal mortality rate has increased over the past decade, despite legalizing abortion in 1997. Finally, Chile, which criminalized abortion in 1989, has had a steadily decreasing maternal mortality rate since then. Rather than abortion being a contributing factor to women's health, Chile's example reveals that increasing levels of education are instrumental in reducing maternal deaths. Similarly, Poland has severe abortion restrictions and has, as of 2015, along with Finland and Greece, the lowest maternal mortality rate in the world (3 deaths per 100 000 births). https://www.cia.gov/library/publications/the-world-factbook/fields/2223.html

5.5 The Solution: Contraception and Birth Control?

The solution pro-choice advocates present as a way to reduce abortion is also deeply flawed. Contraception and sex education, they declare, is the real way to combat abortion rates.

The logic appears to be simple. An increased use of contraception will result in fewer unplanned pregnancies, which in turn will result in fewer abortions. However, the use of contraception as well as increasingly explicit sex-ed curriculums has steadily increased since the introduction of the pill during the 1960s, and so has the abortion rate. If contraception hasn't reduced abortion rates yet, why should we assume it will start working now?

Contraception has never reduced abortion rates. In fact, the boom in availability, acceptance, and use of contraceptives has caused people to develop a disconnect between sex and pregnancy. Many do not consider that the use of their reproductive organs in an act of reproduction may result in them reproducing. While this fact seems elementary, sex-education focuses on the idea of "safe sex," rather than explaining how reproduction works. Sex-ed curriculums emphasize different forms of contraception, leading people to believe that contraception is 100% effective; thus, the disconnect. Contraception has, however, never been completely effective. As a result, when girls or women become pregnant while using faulty contraception, they turn to abortion. Increased use of contraception does not result in decreased abortions; rather, it results in more people having sex, and ultimately, more opportunities for contraception to fail. This information is backed by the leading UK abortion provider, British Pregnancy Advisory Service. They write on their website:

> The answer to unsafe abortion is not contraception, it is safe abortion. When you encourage women to use contraception, you give them the sense that they can control their fertility—but if you do not provide safe abortion services when that contraception fails you are doing them a great disservice. Our data shows women cannot control their fertility through contraception alone, even when they are using some of the most effective   methods. Family planning is contraception and abortion. Abortion is birth control that women need when their regular method lets

them down.[26]

Setting the Record Straight

Plan B: The Morning After Pill

The morning after pill, or plan B, is marketed as an emergency contraceptive. The plan B website declares firmly: "plan B is not an abortion pill—if you take plan B, you will not be terminating a pregnancy." However, only a line above, the third function of this pill is said to: "Prevent a fertilized egg from attaching to the uterus." This reveals the idea that pregnancy begins with implantation, which denies the scientific fact that pregnancy begins days earlier: at fertilization. (Paladin Labs Inc. "How it Works," plan B: THE ORIGINAL MORNING-AFTER PILL, 2015, http://planb.ca/how-it-works.html)

Additionally, not only does contraception use not decrease abortion rates, it results in many early-term abortions. Many contraceptives have abortifacient capabilities. Hormonal birth control methods such as the pill have three functions. First, they discourage ovulation. If no egg is released during a woman's cycle, pregnancy cannot occur. The second function thickens the cervical mucus, making it difficult for

---

26   British Pregnancy Advisory Service. "Women cannot control fertility through contraception alone: bpas data shows 1 in 4 women having an abortion were using most effective contraception." *bpas.* July 7, 2017. https://www.bpas.org/about-our-charity/press-office/press-releases/women-cannot-control-fertility-through-contraception-alone-bpas-data-shows-1-in-4-women-having-an-abortion-were-using-most-effective-contraception/.

sperm to travel to the fallopian tubes, effectively preventing fertilization. The third function is a "back-up plan" for if the first two functions fail. The majority of birth control methods include this third function, which thins the uterine lining. This acts as an abortifacient, since any embryo that is conceived (despite the use of contraception) will likely be unable to implant in the uterine lining,[27] and this results in the death of that tiny human being. There is no way to calculate just how many abortions contraceptives have caused, but it is sure to be no small number.

5.6 Conclusion

We live in a world where reality is often difficult to face. It is understandable that people often scramble to create grey areas in order to justify actions that appear to be the easiest escape from a difficult situation. However, as pro-lifers, we must be consistent in our reasoning. It is not compassionate to give up ground; it is the opposite, as countless women are hurt by this, and countless children will die. We can be both consistent and compassionate for two reasons. First, the truth is on our side. There are logical arguments that we can present to each of these seemingly "grey" situations, and there is reliable research for these arguments to stand firm on. But equally important is the fact that to be truly compassionate, we must seek the best for others. Abortion is never the best option for the mother or her child. The abortion procedure violently destroys the pre-born child and is damaging to women and their families. We will explore this fact in depth in the next chapter.

---

27   Melissa Conrad Stöppler, MD, "Hormonal Methods of Birth Control," MedicineNet.com, February 2, 2015, https://www.medicinenet.com/hormonal_ methods_of_birth_control/article.htm.

Key Takeaways

- When speaking about the question of abortion in cases of sexual assault, we need to evaluate the situation before we respond. We can respond with:

    - a question: **In a country where we don't give the death penalty to the guilty rapist, why do we give it to the innocent child?**

    - by **trotting out the toddler**

- When talking about terminal pre-natal diagnosis, we need to emphasize that all human beings have the right to life, regardless of how long that life may be. **When we have only a short time left with a loved one, we maximize that time, rather than cutting it short.**

- When speaking about the question of the life of the mother we need to recall:

    - **The Dublin Declaration:** Abortion is never medically necessary to save a woman's life.

    - **The Principle of Double Effect:**

        1. *the evil effect is not intended as a means or an end, and*

        2. *there is a proportionately serious reason for allowing the evil effect.*

    - **The drowning people analogy**

- Abortion restrictions do have a positive effect on

Key Takeaways - *continued*

abortion rates.

- The numbers regarding maternal mortality and abortion have been greatly exaggerated. If a procedure is not moral, we have no right to try to make it safe.

- Contraception and birth control do not effectively reduce abortion rates. Hormonal forms of contraception and birth control can function as abortifacients.

5.7 Diving Deeper

1. Why is it important not to have exceptions to our pro-life stance? What do allowances for abortion in certain circumstances say about the pre-born? Why do you think some people have exceptions?

2. There are situations in pregnancy where a doctor may recommend abortion as the only way of saving someone's life. What is this person's responsibility in this difficult situation? How does this question illustrate the importance of knowing why we believe what we believe from a young age?

3. We know that abortion restrictions do make a difference,

but if restrictions really did have no affect on abortion rates, what should we do? Is this a good argument for having no restrictions at all? How could we go about making sure that these restrictions are, in fact, effective?

5.8 Suggested Activities

1. View the videos *Choosing Thomas* and *99 Balloons*. What quotes stood out to you as you were watching? Discuss how these stories help us see the importance of choosing life, no matter how difficult the circumstances.

2. Ask a friend or family member what they think about abortion. If they are pro-life, ask them if they have any exceptions to their position, and if so, why. Use the apologetics you learned in this chapter to explain why exceptions are unnecessary.

3. Research the maternal mortality rates of different countries. Then research their abortion laws. What do you find? What is more indicative of positive change: abortion or better healthcare?

5.9 Additional Resources

- Brandon Bosma: Incompatible with Life (*https://www.youtube.com/watch?v=bzPK4Kjtxuk*)

  - This Ted Talk by Brandon Bosma shows how a diagnosis that claims a child is 'incompatible with life' can be inaccurate, and how living with certain conditions is possible.

- Choosing Thomas (*https://www.youtube.com/watch?v=ToNWquoXqJI*), and 99 Balloons (*https://www.youtube.com/watch?v=th6Njr-qkq0*)

- These videos tell the powerful stories of two children, Thomas and Elliot, and their families. Thomas and Elliot were given terminal diagnosis while in-utero, and while their parents were offered abortions, they chose life.

- Canadian Physicians for Life: https://www.physiciansforlife.ca

  - This website offers different resources discussion questions of maternal health, contraception, etc.

Part Six: The Abortion Procedure

Discussing the humanity of pre-born children does not reveal the brutality of abortion.

"When it was done, I felt a sudden emptiness and knew I had made the worst mistake of my life. It's with me every day, and all I can do is wonder. I wonder how my baby would've looked, I wonder what would've been my baby's favourite colour, and I wonder if I would have had a baby boy or a baby girl.
The abortion has changed my life completely. I'd do anything and give anything just to have my baby back inside of me—growing day by day."
20-year old post-abortive woman

6.1 Introduction

It was a small, unassuming, red brick building—the kind of building that people drive past without even noticing that it's there. While its appearance boasted of nothing, on a cool day in February, I was standing, facing this building, and waiting. Time went slowly, and the thought crossed my mind: *Maybe no one is coming.* In this case, that would be a good thing.

The first girl hurried up the drive. She was slightly bent over and refused to make eye contact. A sidewalk counsellor reached out and offered to help her, but she hurried to the front door and disappeared inside. I felt sick. More women followed. Some were laughing and talking with friends, clutching onto their arms tightly. Some were led by boyfriends who hurried them through the front door, sending glares over their shoulders to those of us on the sidewalk. One woman was propelled forward by a heavily tattooed man with a cigarette dangling from one hand. She resisted his efforts to have her ignore us, and stopped. With one hand rubbing her swollen abdomen she called out, "Have you come to witness my child sacrifice?"

It was as if a cold fist had tightened around my stomach. *It wasn't true. It couldn't be true.* And yet, it was. I realized then, that up until that moment I had not been able to believe that women actually went through with having an abortion. The idea was so foreign and so distasteful that I had never been able to completely face the horror of it. As I stood with fellow volunteers on the sidewalk in front of that abortion clinic, I was sick with the knowledge that there was only a thin layer of brick and plaster between myself and a man who was calmly shredding tiny arms, tiny legs, and tiny bodies with metal forceps and a suction machine. At that moment abortion was never more real to me, and I have never felt so helpless.

The women that crept out of the clinic hours later were

not laughing and talking. They gripped brown paper bags in their hands, containing medication they had to take the next day. Even the woman who had so boldly laughed at us was sober as she exited the building. We all knew what had taken place there. We *knew,* and no loud, false laughter or empty chatter could take away the weight of that knowledge.

6.2 Why is it important to talk about this?

It is a scientific fact that pre-born children are living human beings, a fact that is demonstrable through simple questions. The outcome of the abortion debate largely depends on the understanding society has of the humanity of pre-born children, and the pro-life case is completely logical. However, the response people have to the subject of abortion is often more emotional than logical. This means that we have to approach the issue with compassion, which we will discuss in Part Seven, but it also indicates another important point that must be made. People view abortion as a good solution in a difficult circumstance. However, the abortion procedure itself is extremely disturbing, and once the barbarity of abortion is discussed, it is hard for anyone to see it as a truly good solution.

It is important to note that were the procedure not brutal, it would still be wrong. Even if we found a way to dispose of human beings in a completely clean and painless way, the act itself would still be immoral. It is for this reason that understanding what abortion entails is not our most powerful tool in discussion. However, when the horror of abortion is understood, it inspires empathy with the victims in a way that logical arguments do not. While many assert that choice is important, it is often difficult for them not to recoil when they consider exactly what is being chosen.

For the most part, our society accepts abortion, and even

celebrates it. This is possible because it goes on behind sterile clinic doors. It is possible to deny the humanity of the pre-born child because no one is forced to consider who that child is. Pre-born children are declared to be just "clumps of cells," a group of tissue that is removed from a woman's uterus that is not nor looks anything like a human being. While science illustrates that whether we look like human beings is irrelevant to whether we actually *are* human beings, the fact is that pre-born children *do* have the physical characteristics we recognize as human from very early in their development. It is beneficial to discuss how abortions are performed and how the life of a developing child is ended, precisely because many people are completely unaware of these facts. Where logic fails to convince, the stark reality of the horrific nature of abortion often persuades people that this is not something they can support.

6.3 First-Trimester Abortion

The first trimester of pregnancy is measured from fertilization to week twelve of fetal development. During this stage of pregnancy, there are two abortion procedures that are offered.

A. Medical Abortion

A medical abortion can only be done in the first trimester. It is recommended as it is less invasive than any of the surgical procedures. The Planned Parenthood website explains that people may choose a medical abortion because

> "you can have your medication abortion at home or in another comfortable place that you choose. You get to decide who you want to be with during your abortion, or you can go it alone. Because medication abortion is similar to miscarriage, many people feel

like it's more 'natural.'"[1]

Medical abortion, which is also known as the abortion pill, has been available in Europe for over twenty-five years, and it has been legal in the United States since the year 2000. There have been complications—taking an abortion pill with an undiagnosed ectopic pregnancy can be fatal—but for the most part medical abortion is safe for women, though, of course, it is never safe for their pre-born children. Due to certain complications, Health Canada has advised that medical abortions be prescribed only by a doctor, or, in some provinces, by a nurse practitioner. It is also recommended that the first step in the procedure—taking the first pill—should be done in a doctor's office or primary care clinic. The rationale for this is that the abortion pill is unsafe for women if they use corticosteroids (medication resembling the hormone cortisol), have an ectopic pregnancy, ovarian mass, IUD, adrenal failure, anemia, bleeding disorders or use of blood thinners, asthma, liver or kidney problems, heart disease, or high blood pressure, some of which can only be determined by medical examination. It is important to note that if any of these conditions are undiagnosed and a woman attempts to medically abort on her own, her health could be seriously compromised.

The abortion pill in Canada is sold under the name Mifegymiso. Mifegymiso is a two-step drug regimen. The pill taken in the doctor's office contains Mifepristone, which may be better known as RU-486. Mifepristone blocks the production of the hormone progesterone, which stabilizes the lining of the uterus in order to make it a habitable place for the early embryo. Without adequate progesterone, the lining of the uterus breaks down, no longer sustaining the pre-born child attached to it. In the early stages of a medical abortion, this process can

---

1   Planned Parenthood, "The Abortion Pill," *plannedparenthood.org*, 2017, https://www.plannedparenthood.org/learn/abortion/the-abortion-pill.

be reversed and the pre-born child saved, if progesterone is administered on time.[2] In fact, in 2018 Heartbeat International reported that more than 500 babies have been born as a result of this procedure, known as abortion pill reversal.[3]

However, in most cases Mifepristone successfully breaks down the uterine lining, resulting in the death of the embryo. The second step of the abortion requires an additional pill to be ingested between 24 to 48 hours after Mifepristone was administered. This pill contains Misoprostol, also called Zitotec 200, which together with the Mifepristone creates severe cramping and contractions, often accompanied by heavy bleeding, to expel the baby from the uterus. This process usually lasts around five hours, but it could last up to 24.[4]

Medical abortions are recommended up to the 49th day of pregnancy but can be used up to nine weeks. However, the later this type of abortion is attempted, the more likely it is to fail. The failure rate at seven weeks and below is at 5%, whereas the failure rate for nine weeks is 10%. If the medical abortion is unsuccessful in ending the life of the pre-born child, a woman is offered a surgical abortion.

The complications for a medical abortion, along with the cramping, can include heavy bleeding, which causes 1% of women to require hospitalization. Women often feel nauseous, dizzy, and can have diarrhea. They may also experience abdominal pain and vomiting.[5]

---

2   Live Action, "Abortion Procedures: What You need to Know, Abortion Pills," abortionprocedures.com, 2016, https://www.abortionprocedures.com/abortion-pill/.

3   Franklin, Katie. "Over 500 Babies Born Thanks to Abortion Pill Reversal," *pregnancy help news,* October 2018, https://pregnancyhelpnews.com/over-500-babies-born-thanks-to-abortion-pill-reversal/.

4   Planned Parenthood, "The Abortion Pill," *plannedparenthood.org,* 2017, https://www.plannedparenthood.org/learn/abortion/the-abortion-pill.

5   Ibid.

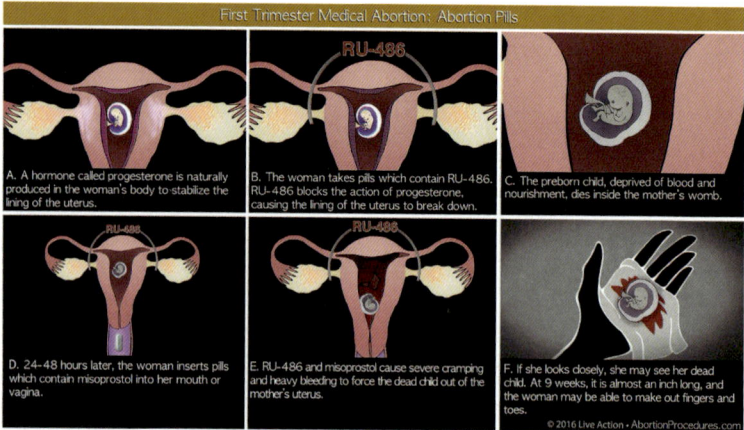

First Trimester Medical Abortion: Abortion Pills

A. A hormone called progesterone is naturally produced in the woman's body to stabilize the lining of the uterus.

B. The woman takes pills which contain RU-486. RU-486 blocks the action of progesterone, causing the lining of the uterus to break down.

C. The preborn child, deprived of blood and nourishment, dies inside the mother's womb.

D. 24-48 hours later, the woman inserts pills which contain misoprostol into her mouth or vagina.

E. RU-486 and misoprostol cause severe cramping and heavy bleeding to force the dead child out of the mother's uterus.

F. If she looks closely, she may see her dead child. At 9 weeks, it is almost an inch long, and the woman may be able to make out fingers and toes.

© 2016 Live Action • AbortionProcedures.com

Figure 6.1 *Medical Abortion*   *www.abortionprocedures.com*

B. Surgical Abortion

A first-trimester surgical abortion is the most frequently conducted abortion. It is a same-day procedure that lasts from five to ten minutes, though most women will still spend several hours in the clinic. People usually prefer this procedure to a medical abortion, as it is done in a clinic with doctors and nurses on hand, and only local anesthesia is necessary. A surgical abortion is most often performed as a Manual Vacuum Aspiration (MVA). In an MVA procedure a woman's cervix is anaesthetized and then dilated using a series of metal rods. Then, a suction catheter is inserted into the uterus through the vagina. The suction is powerful, emptying the uterus of the amniotic fluid and placenta, and shredding the tiny pre-born child. In some cases, this procedure has an extra step, where a curette—a rod with a circular head—is used to scrape the walls of the uterus to ensure that it is completely empty. In Canada, an MVA is most commonly performed between 8-12 weeks. The most serious complication associated with this procedure is infection, which is caused when parts of the baby or placenta are left inside the uterus after the abortion is complete, or from the surgical invasion of the uterus by medical equipment. Another common and potentially serious complication is excessive vaginal bleeding post procedure due to retained embryo or placental tissue.[6]

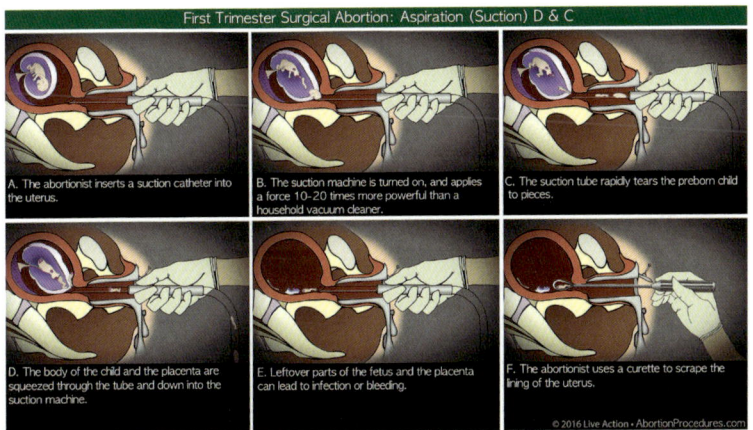

Figure 6.2 *MVA Abortion*   *www.abortionprocedures.com*

6.4 Second-Trimester Abortion

A. Dilation and Curettage (D & C)

For an early second-trimester abortion, from twelve to sixteen weeks, the procedure most often used is very similar to a first-trimester MVA, called a Dilation and Curettage (D & C). However, because the baby develops so quickly during the initial weeks of pregnancy, a second trimester abortion always entails the use of a curette to scrape the walls of the uterus to ensure that no parts of the baby's body remain inside.

---

6   Perry, S. E., Hockenberry, et al. (2013). *Maternal child nursing care in Canada* (1st ed.). Toronto, Canada: Elsevier Mosby.

B. Dilation and Evacuation (D & E)

A Dilation and Evacuation (D & E) abortion is generally performed between 14-16 weeks gestation, but can be performed up to 20 weeks. At this point, the pre-born child is anywhere from 3.5 inches to 8 inches long and will not fit down the suction catheter. A D & E is performed under anaesthesia and if it is a later-term abortion the cervix needs to be prepared several hours or days in advance with laminaria. Laminaria is a type of sterilized seaweed that is inserted into the vagina. The sticks of seaweed absorb moisture from the woman's body and expand, forcing the cervix open. Misoprostol may also be applied to the cervix. Once the cervix is sufficiently dilated, the abortionist uses a vacuum aspirator to suction out the amniotic fluid surrounding and protecting the pre-born child.

After the amniotic fluid is removed, the abortionist uses forceps, also called a sopher clamp, to dismember the pre-born child. Forceps are grasping instruments, long and slender, with two-inch clamps at the end outfitted with sharp teeth. Once the forceps are inserted into the uterus, they grip the child's arm or leg, twist, and pull to remove it. After the baby's limbs and body is dismembered and removed from the uterus, the abortionist feels about for the child's head and crushes it. A white fluid—the baby's brains—then flows from the woman's vagina. A curette is used to remove the placenta and any remaining body parts. After the abortion is complete, the baby must be pieced back together to make sure that no parts of his or her tiny body remain inside the woman's body.

This type of abortion procedure has more complications than first-trimester abortions. The uterus may be perforated, or the cervix lacerated by the sharp instruments used, risking long-term cervical damage. There is also a risk of infection or hemorrhage.

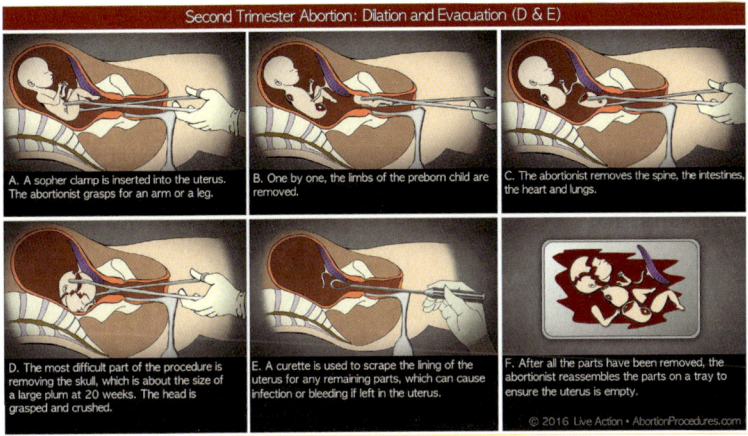

Figure 6.3 *D & E Abortion*   *www.abortionprocedures.com*

6.5 Third-Trimester Abortion

Third-trimester abortions are rare. The majority of Canadians are uncomfortable with the idea of a completely viable child being killed within the womb, and there are very few Canadian doctors willing to carry out the procedure. However, it is legal, and due to the absence of reporting requirements, there is no way to know how often it happens. Still, we know that it *does* happen, as evidenced by the Montreal couple who sought an abortion at 30 weeks in 2016. They were refused by two hospitals before they received the desired abortion at 35 weeks gestation. Most women seeking this procedure must go to the United States, and the Montreal Gazette reporting on the couples' story claimed that "an estimated 17 to 42 Quebec women go south every year to terminate a third-trimester pregnancy."[7] Third-trimester abortions take two to three days due to the size of

---

7   Charlie Fidelman, "Montreal woman who had late abortion says she made the right decision," *Montreal Gazette,* December 23, 2016, http://montrealgazette.com/news/local-news/montreal-woman-who-had-late-abortion-says-she-made-the-right-decision.

the pre-born child. At this point in their development, pre-born children can feel pain as acutely as any born human being.[8]

A. Induction Procedure: Injection and Stillbirth

The first step of the induction procedure involves injecting the pre-born child with digoxin or potassium chloride. A high enough dose of either of these drugs will result in cardiac arrest. A long needle is used to puncture the baby's head or torso, either through the woman's abdomen or vagina. After the cardiotoxic drug is administered, the abortionist must dilate the cervix. This may be done by inserting laminaria or a balloon catheter into the woman's vagina, or by using prostaglandins. Because of the size of the child at this point and how tightly the woman's cervix is closed, dilation takes a significant amount of time. After the cervix is prepped for dilation, the woman returns home or to her hotel to wait.

On the second day of the procedure, the woman returns to the clinic and the laminaria is replaced. Sometimes a second ultrasound is conducted, and if the pre-born child is still alive a second dose of digoxin is administered. One of the most feared "side effects" of late-term abortion is what is called "live birth." If the child is not successfully killed within the womb, the abortionist has a problem on their hands. Therefore, every precaution must be taken to ensure that this does not happen. Once again, the woman returns home.

At any point during this procedure, a woman may go into labour. If she is unable to get to the clinic on time, she may be forced to deliver her dead child into a toilet. Additionally, this procedure usually involves the woman carrying her dead child within her for two or three days. If the child is not

---

8   Claire Chretien, "Babies can feel the abortionist ripping them apart: here's the scientific evidence," *Life Site News, https://www.lifesitenews.com/blogs/the-scientific-evidence-that-babies-feel-pain-as-they-are-aborted.*

delivered whole, the doctor must perform a D & E in order to remove all the pieces of the child and prevent infection.

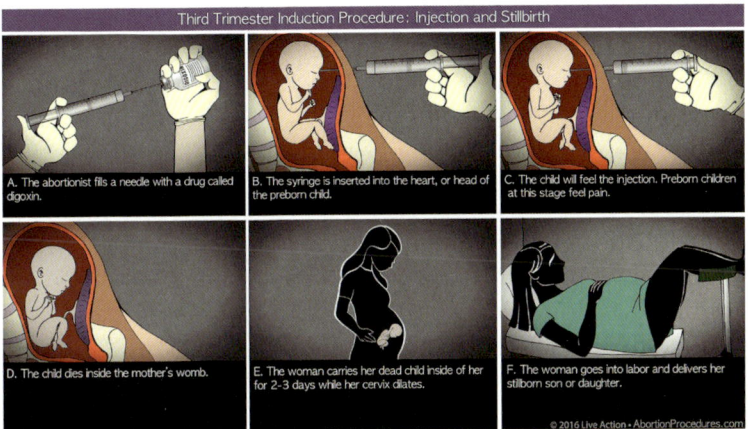

Figure 6.4 *Induction Procedure*   *www.abortionprocedures.com*

B. Intact Dilation and Extraction (D & X)

Intact Dilation and Extraction (D & X) is the notorious partial-birth abortion procedure. This procedure is done when a pregnancy is in its latest stages. Sometimes digoxin is injected into the child as an initial step, and the cervix is dilated in the same way that it is for the induction procedure. At times misoprostol is also used to soften the cervix.

When it is time for the procedure to take place, the child is delivered feet first. The abortionist then uses their left hand to grip the shoulders of the baby and slides a closed scissors up until they reach the base of the skull. After making sure the scissors are in the right position, the scissors are thrust into the baby's head and then opened to break open the skull. A suction catheter is inserted and the child's brains are suctioned out. The dead child is then completely removed from the birth canal.

Because third-trimester abortions are so late term, the risk of complication is greatly increased from that of a second-trimester abortion. Both procedures described have a high risk of hemorrhage, lacerations, and uterine perforations, all of which can and have led to maternal death.

Testimony Spotlight

While sharing the truth of what abortion is, a group of young teenagers called out to me, yelling that they thought abortion was amazing. I walked over to them.

"Hey guys," I said. "Do you know what abortion really is?"

"It's a great thing!" they enthused.

"But do you know what it really does?" I asked again.

"No," they admitted.

I described abortion to them, step by gruesome step: the dismembering, the skull-crushing, the suction aspirator. By the time I had finished, each one had grown pale and silent.

~ Jonathon Van Maren

C. Medical Induction or Medical Interruption of Pregnancy

Due to under-reporting of abortions in North America, it's difficult to say for certain, but it is likely that another type of procedure is more common for late second-trimester and third trimester abortions, namely a medical induction or medical interruption of pregnancy. This procedure is generally performed for parents with children who have been diagnosed with a disability, deformity, or serious health condition. In these situations, labour is induced late in the second trimester or early in the third. Parents sign a DNR order (do not resuscitate), and so the tiny child is left to die.

6.6 Abortion and Women

A. *Abortion is wrong because it hurts women*

In the past, pro-lifers have often argued that abortion is wrong because it hurts women. While it is true that the abortion procedure can result in various complications and leave long-term psychological damage, there are two fundamental problems with this argument. The first problem is a practical one; with every story of a negative experience with abortion, there is a positive abortion story to counter it. When someone declares that they regret their abortion deeply, other women inevitably state that abortion changed their lives for the better. Even some women who have been subject to adverse physical affects as a result of their abortion defend it, claiming that pregnancy and childbirth would have been worse. Abortion does hurt women—it is an invasive procedure that violently interrupts a healthy, natural process—and this fact is important to the abortion debate. Women and men who bravely step forward to share how abortion has devastated their lives are important to the pro-life movement, particularly in the area of post-abortion counselling. However, this cannot be the foundation of our position.

The second reason we should not rely on this argument is even more important; abortion is not wrong because it hurts women, abortion is wrong because it ends the life of an innocent human being. Abortion harms women precisely *because* it ends the life of their child. Pregnancy is a natural process during which the body produces hormones that form the foundation of a nurturing relationship between mother and child. It is for this reason that losing a baby through miscarriage is such a tragedy. Abortion, on the other hand, is entirely unnatural, and its effects are often difficult for women to deal with psychologically. Both the adverse physical and mental effects abortion can have are awful, but they are not the primary reason why we so urgently need to speak out against abortion. While the abortion procedure itself rarely threatens the life of a woman, it always has tragic results for her pre-born child.

B. Is abortion safer than pregnancy and child-birth?

When the potential complications of abortion are pointed out—complications Planned Parenthood itself admits could happen[9]—a popular pro-abortion counter-argument is that abortion is very safe, safer, in fact, than pregnancy and child-birth. In other words, if women considered whether to continue a pregnancy on the basis of health alone, abortion would be their best option. Although this claim has been thoroughly debunked, like so many other tired abortion arguments it is still embraced by the abortion rights movement.

The first problem with this claim is one that anyone who bothers to do any research would easily find. The basis for this argument rests in the comparison of the data resulting from studies on maternal mortality and abortion mortality done by the Centers for Disease Control (CDC). These numbers show that there is a higher maternal mortality rate than abortion mortality rate, a fact pro-choice advocates cite with great satisfaction. However, the CDC itself has pointed out that these numbers are not comparable. A letter

---

9   Planned Parenthood, "How safe is an in-clinic abortion?" plannedparenthood.org, 2017, https://www.plannedparenthood.org/learn/abortion/in-clinic-abortion-procedures/how-safe-is-an-in-clinic-abortion.

written by Julie Gerberding, Director of the CDC, states that the "measures are conceptually different and are used by the CDC for different health purposes,"[10] which means that holding these numbers beside each other is not comparing like to like.

The Amicus Brief of the American Center for Law and Justice's report written to answer the question of whether these points are comparable explains why they are not. It points out that the way in which the maternal mortality rate is determined does not take into account miscarriage, stillbirth, or even abortion. The CDC divides the number of maternal deaths by live births, rather than by pregnancies. This means that women who die as a result of complications associated with pregnancy or miscarriage will be counted as maternal deaths, while the women who survive miscarriage or stillbirth won't factor into the live births.[11] This naturally inflates the maternal death numbers.

Not only are the numbers incomparable because of how maternal mortality is measured, abortion mortality is extremely difficult to calculate. First of all, in both Canada and the United States there are no federal reporting requirements,[12] which means that any information on the effects of abortion are only estimates. Various states have

---

10   Thomas P. Monaghan, et al. "Alberto R. Gonzales, Attorney General, v. Planned Parenthood Federation of America, et al., Amicus Brief of the American Center for Law and Justice in Support of Petitioner," *American Center for Law and Justice*, no. 05-1382 (2006): 4. http://www.findlawimages.com/efile/supreme/briefs/05-1382/05-1382.mer.ami.aclj.pdf.

11   Thomas P. Monaghan, et al. "Alberto R. Gonzales, Attorney General, v. Planned Parenthood Federation of America, et al., Amicus Brief of the American Center for Law and Justice in Support of Petitioner," *American Center for Law and Justice*, no. 05-1382 (2006): 5. http://www.findlawimages.com/efile/supreme/briefs/05-1382/05-1382.mer.ami.aclj.pdf.

12   Elizabeth Ring-Cassidy & Ian Gentles, *Women's Health after Abortion: The Medical and Psychological Evidence Second Edition* (Toronto: The deVeber Institute for Bioethics and Social Research), 7.

moved to implement mandatory reporting laws in order to obtain accurate information about the effects of the abortion procedure. However, "concerns about the potential risks of retaliation against abortion providers or violation of the medical privacy of women obtaining abortions have played a role in debates over the scope and specificity of abortion reporting."[13] This hesitancy has resulted in the vast majority of abortion reporting being completely voluntary, and, as a result, consistently unreliable.

The Guttmacher Institute, which is the organization other than the CDC that collects abortion data, admits that, "Abortions are underreported at different rates both between and within populations," and further, that "estimates of abortion, contraceptive failure, miscarriage and reproductive histories that rely on self-reports are all subject to bias by abortion underreporting, and the extent of bias in each case is unknown."[14] The likely fallout of this lack of research "is an overly favourable assessment of health risks due to abortion since women often do not report their abortion history."[15]

Voluntary reporting results in inaccurate data due to bias, and further, the data that is available is severely limited. Abortion providers are reluctant to provide information because of the controversial nature of this issue, and despite all the efforts of the pro-choice movement to encourage women to trumpet their abortion experience, many women view abortion as an unpleasant experience best forgotten.

---

13   Charles A. Donovan & Nora Sullivan, "Abortion Reporting Laws: Tears in the Fabric," *American Reports Series* no. 3 (2012): 9, https://www.scribd.com/document/117449628/Abortion-Reporting-Laws-Tears-in-the-Fabric#.

14   J. Richard Udry, et al., "A Medical Record Linkage Analysis of Abortion Underreporting," *Perspectives On Sexual And Reproductive Health: A journal of peer-reviewed research* 28, no. 5 (1996): 228, doi: https://doi.org/10.1363/2822896.

15   Byron Calhoun, "The maternal mortality myth in the context of legalized abortion," *The Linacre Quarterly* 80, no. 3 (2013): 266, doi: 10.1179/2050854913Y.0000000004.

As a result, "less than half of all abortions [are] reported by women in face-to-face interviews."[16]

Because women often neglect to report their abortions, abortion does not appear in their medical records. This is crucial to understanding why abortion mortality rates are extremely difficult to calculate. When women experience complications as a result of the abortion procedure, they do not return to the abortion clinic. Rather, they are sent to "local emergency rooms to be seen by other health care providers."[17] This means that "for various reasons . . . deaths due to abortion are often not recorded as resulting from the procedure, with only the immediate cause of death (e.g., embolism, sepsis, and hemorrhage) provided."[18] In fact, this may even result in these deaths being recorded as maternal deaths, further skewing the numbers.[19] The total lack of information, as well as the way in which the measures are determined, means that no pro-abortion advocate can build a solid case built on statistics; the statistics are either unreliable or unavailable.

A final important point proving the argument that abortion is safer than pregnancy and childbirth is a myth, is that what reporting is available "tends to be limited to short-term complications."[20] Short-term refers to the time

16   Ibid.

17   Ibid.

18   Byron Calhoun, "The maternal mortality myth in the context of legalized abortion," *The Linacre Quarterly* 80, no. 3 (2013): 267, doi: 10.1179/2050854913Y.0000000004.

19   Kaczor, Christopher Robert. *The Ethics of Abortion: Women's Rights, Human Life, and the Question of Justice.* 2015. [WorldCat: https://www.worldcat.org/title/ethics-of-abortion-womens-rights-human-life-and-the-question-of-justicethe-ethics-of-abortion-womens-rights-human-life-and-the-question-of-justice/oclc/900886181&referer=brief_results]

20   Elizabeth Ring-Cassidy & Ian Gentles, *Women's Health after Abortion: The Medical and Psychological Evidence Second Edition* (Toronto: The deVeber Institute for Bioethics and Social Research), 5.

spent by the woman in the abortion clinic. As soon as she leaves the premises, "it is unclear precisely what happens when complications emerge several days or weeks later. For the most part it appears that the diagnosis and treatment of following issues are left to community hospitals or family physicians," which means that the link to abortion may never be drawn.[21] In fact, when asked, few doctors actually knew that their patients have had an abortion. In the *Survey of Canadian Physicians on Women's Health after Induced Abortion*, the responses to the question, "Do hospitals or clinics in your area notify you if one of your patients has had an induced abortion?" clearly delineates the glaring problems with abortion reporting. Of the 179 physicians asked this question, "107 said no, 48 said yes, and 24 were unsure."[22]

Ultimately, long-term risks that only manifest themselves during subsequent pregnancies or later in life are rarely connected to abortion. In no other common medical procedure is there so little information, and no other procedure is seen through such rose-colored lenses. The fact is that "the lifelong risks of repeat, induced, and late-term abortions on women's health are not being addressed in the research literature,"[23] and as a result, women are not being given pertinent information regarding their health and safety.

C. *Legal abortion is a safe, painless procedure*

Pro-choice advocates often state that legal abortion is safe and painless. Looking at the procedure itself and the time it takes to be completed, this statement is fairly accurate. Like all medical procedures, abortion has its risks to the women, risks that grow depending on how late in

---

21   Ibid., 7
22   Ibid., 6
23   Ibid., 5.

pregnancy an abortion is performed. Abortion is not a painless procedure, as women experience varying degrees of cramping as a result. However, it is true that abortion is relatively safe in the immediate time in which it is taking place. However, pro-choice advocates have shown telling reluctance in their willingness to research long-term risks.

Abortion has become such a politicized issue that any information regarding adverse long-term effects of abortion is decried by pro-choice advocates as pro-life propaganda. This unsettling truth was uncovered by pro-choice director Punam Kumar Gill, who released a documentary in 2016, aptly named *HUSH*. She describes her surprise at the general unwillingness of mainstream researchers to acknowledge obvious links between abortion and breast cancer, pre-term birth, and psychological trauma. She spoke to Dr. David Grimes, a well-respected OBGYN and abortionist, and when asked if there were any long-term effects of abortion he stated firmly, "What we now know is that there are no long-term consequences from abortion either reproductive or otherwise, and that includes psychological effects as well."[24] This information was repeated to Gill at an abortion clinic, where she was told that the link between abortion and breast cancer specifically was a myth. This is echoed on the Planned Parenthood website, where the answer to the question, "Does abortion have long-term side effects?" definitively declares:

> "Having an abortion doesn't increase your risk for breast cancer or affect your fertility. It doesn't cause problems for future pregnancies like birth defects, premature birth or low birth weight, ectopic

---

24   *Hush: A Liberating Conversation About Abortion and Women's Health,* directed by Punam Kumar Gill (Mighty Motion Pictures, 2016), DVD.

pregnancy, miscarriage, or infant death."[25]

However, many studies from around the world do find a statistically significant link between abortion and all of the complications Planned Parenthood listed. If this is the case, where is the research? The pro-choice movement has done an excellent job in concealing information and crucifying anyone who dares to contradict them. Any pro-life researcher or physician attempting to present studies is dismissed as an anti-abortion zealot. This cover-up frustrates many who are simply trying to help people, such as Dr. Angela Lanfranchi, a breast surgeon interviewed by Gill. With tears in her eyes, Dr. Lanfranchi relayed that while she had been relieved initially when studies were put forward linking abortion with breast cancer, she was consistently disappointed: "Over the years I realized that, no, it didn't matter how many studies there were. That information was not going to get out."[26]

Dr. Lanfranchi was upset because women are dying not due to a lack of information, but because the information is not accurately presented to them. Multiple studies have been produced, showing that the hormone *oestradiol*, which is released during the first trimester, triggers "an explosive growth of breast tissue, [during] a period when breast cells are most likely to be affected by carcinogens."[27] When the pregnancy is unnaturally ended, this immature breast tissue leaves many more places for cancer to grow. Researchers have accurately predicted a country's breast cancer rate

25   Planned Parenthood, "How safe is an in-clinic abortion?" plannedparenthood.org, 2017, https://www.plannedparenthood.org/learn/abortion/in-clinic-abortion-procedures/how-safe-is-an-in-clinic-abortion.
26   *Hush: A Liberating Conversation About Abortion and Women's Health,* directed by Punam Kumar Gill (Mighty Motion Pictures, 2016), DVD.
27   Elizabeth Ring-Cassidy & Ian Gentles, *Women's Health after Abortion: The Medical and Psychological Evidence Second Edition* (Toronto: The deVeber Institute for Bioethics and Social Research), 18.

based on their abortion rate.[28] In China, where up until recently the one-child policy was rigorously enforced through abortion, breast cancer rates are skyrocketing.

When Gill investigated why the medical establishment states so conclusively that there are no long-term effects from abortion, she discovered that the decision was based on a single conference that took place in 2003. This conference was put on by the National Health Organization's cancer division. The decision that abortion and breast cancer were not linked was made by a handful of researchers, after hearing a single 20-minute presentation by cancer researcher Dr. Leslie Bernstein. Ever since then, the medical establishment has declared the case closed.

The same sort of cover-up is applied to other health risks, such as pre-term birth. During a surgical abortion, a woman's cervix is forced open with metal rods called dilators, or, in late-term abortions, with laminaria. This action can weaken the cervix to the point where it is not able to support a subsequent full-term pregnancy. Again, the medical establishment refuses to look into a possible link between abortion and the spike in premature births happening in the Western World.

Perhaps the boldest claim abortion advocates make is that abortion produces no adverse psychological effects. The media publicizes campaigns such as the "1 in 3" and "Shout Your Abortion," where women are encouraged to proudly declare their abortion experiences as empowering life decisions. On the other hand, the Silent No More Awareness Campaign, where thousands of women and other relatives of abortion victims have told their stories of regret and heartbreak, is largely dismissed as more "pro-life

---

28   *Hush: A Liberating Conversation About Abortion and Women's Health,* directed by Punam Kumar Gill (Mighty Motion Pictures, 2016), DVD.

propaganda." At pro-life events, protestors often shout down women who are trying to express the regret they feel due to their abortions.[29] While women who claim that abortion was the best decision they ever made are celebrated, the experiences of women who say that their abortion haunts them every hour of every day are completely invalidated.

Personal experience with abortion is largely subjective. There are most likely just as many women who claim that abortion was a positive experience for them as there are women who express profound regret. Further, a lack of long-term research makes it difficult to determine for certain what kind of psychological effects abortion has. However, as David Reardon points out, when people were fighting for abortion to be legalized, the claim was that abortion would reduce levels of mental illness, as fewer girls would have to struggle through unplanned pregnancies. However, the opposite has been the case; mental illness has been on the rise over the past decades.[30] Priscilla Coleman, a Professor of Human Development and Family Studies, references the fact that, "Research has systematically shown that women who have had an abortion are at a higher risk for substance abuse, anxiety, depression, suicidal type thoughts and behaviours, [and] eating disorders . . ."[31] A prestigious study in Finland "discovered *a suicide rate among women who aborted nearly six times greater than among women who delivered their babies.*"[32] Despite the extensive nature of much of this research, it goes largely ignored.

---

29   Katie Yoder, "Media adore '1 in 3 Campaign,' censor women who regret abortion," *LifeSite News,* December 3, 2014, https://www.lifesitenews.com/opinion/media-adore-1-in-3-campaign-censor-women-who-regret-abortion.

30   *Hush: A Liberating Conversation About Abortion and Women's Health,* directed by Punam Kumar Gill (Mighty Motion Pictures, 2016), DVD.

31   Ibid.

32   Elizabeth Ring-Cassidy & Ian Gentles, *Women's Health after Abortion: The Medical and Psychological Evidence Second Edition* (Toronto: The deVeber Institute for Bioethics and Social Research), 193.

It is hard to pinpoint abortion as the single causal factor of adverse psychological effects, as women who have abortions are often in negative situations to begin with. Additionally, women often conceal their abortion history, and abortions continue to be underreported. Interestingly, the report by the American Psychological Association that is used to support the claim that abortion has no negative long-term psychological effects makes several admissions. One of these shows that one month after abortion 79% of women claimed that they were satisfied with their decision, while after two years that number dropped to 72%.[33] This means that immediately following their abortion, 21% of women claim that their abortion harmed them more than benefited them. Every year in Canada 100,000 abortions occur, which, according to the statistics, means that 21,000 women feel adverse psychological effects immediately after having an abortion. As time goes on, the number of women suffering as a result of abortion increases.

It is easy to get lost in the statistics, forgetting that each of those 21,000 women have individual stories of pain, hurt, and loss. Abortion is wrong because it ends the life of an innocent human being, but the damage it causes does not end there. Thousands of women and their families suffer deep trauma because they were not given proper information about the risks surrounding abortion.

The important question that needs to be asked is, Why? Why does abortion cause such trauma to women? We know that pre-born children are living human beings that deserve our protection *not in spite* of their vulnerability but *because of it*. Women deserve to know all the information surrounding the abortion procedure, but what they truly need to know is

---

33   Brenda Major, et al., "Report of the APA Task Force on Mental Health and Abortion," *American Psychological Association* (2008): 74, http://www.apa.org/pi/women/programs/abortion/mental-health.pdf

what, or rather *who*, they carry within them.

Testimony Spotlight

Growing up, I knew a girl who later revealed to me that she had had an abortion. At the time, she told me that "it was the best decision I ever made." In the years that followed, she began to have a lot of guilt and anxiety surrounding her abortion. She attended years of therapy, and came to see that her decision to end the life of her child was a very, very bad choice. When I asked her, years later, how she felt about abortion she said, "I wish someone had talked to me about abortion and how it can affect you, especially in the long-term." She felt deep regret that she could not reverse the decision she had made, saying: "Not a day goes by where I don't think about that baby and who she might have become, and then, what I did to her."

~ Charmaine Van Maren

6.7 Conclusion

Pro-choice advocates claim that abortion empowers women to achieve their dreams. They assert that abortion doesn't affect women or society negatively. Abortion just eliminates a clump of cells, they claim, and without this option, women would be unable to succeed in life. These claims are extremely damaging, as all lies are. Pre-born children are living human beings; abortion brutally destroys them. Pregnancy is a healthy and natural process; abortion interrupts this process, which can have long-lasting physical and psychological effects. As pro-choice advocates shriek of empowerment, the tiny bodies of infinitely valuable, unrepeatable children are thrown into dumpsters and incinerators around the world. The negative effects of abortion have seeped into every facet of our society, which is why discussing abortion can be so difficult. Many people have been personally affected in some way by abortion, and that is why having the knowledge to back up our pro-life position is not enough. We must also present the case for life with compassion, which we will explore in Part Seven.

Key Takeaways

- The abortion procedure violently ends the life of an innocent human being. Its brutal reality needs to be exposed.

- First-trimester abortion:

  - Medical abortion: A two-step drug regimen where mifepristone cuts off the production of progesterone and misoprostol induces cramping and bleeding to expel the dead child.

Key Takeaways - *continued*

- Surgical abortion: A Manual Vacuum Aspiration procedure uses a suction aspirator to empty the uterus of the amniotic fluid and placenta, and shreds the pre-born child.

- Second-trimester abortion:

  - From 12-16 weeks a Dilation and Curettage (D & C) procedure is done, which is the same as an MVA, with the addition of a curette scraping the uterus to ensure that there is nothing remaining in the uterus after the procedure is complete.

  - A Dilation and Evacuation abortion is performed after 16 weeks. Suction is used to remove the amniotic fluid, and then the child is systematically dismembered and removed from the uterus.

- Third-trimester abortion:

  - Induction Procedure: A child is injected with digoxin which induces cardiac arrest, after which the child is delivered.

  - Partial birth abortion: A child is delivered feet first. While his/her head remains in the birth canal his/her skull is split open with scissors and the brains are suctioned out.

- Abortion is not wrong because it harms women, it is wrong because it ends the life of a pre-born child.

Key Takeaways - *continued*

- Abortion is not safer than pregnancy and childbirth. Its long-term effects are impossible to compute due to a lack of reporting requirements and the skillful concealment of stats by the pro-choice movement.

- Pre-born children have decidedly human characteristics from the earliest stages of pregnancy.

6.8 Diving Deeper

1. In reading about the different abortion procedures, do you think one is worse than another? Why is it important to talk about *every* type of abortion, not just those that happen in later trimesters?

2. Knowing that abortionists literally have to piece the bodies of babies back together to ensure that they have successfully completed an abortion, how do you think those who work in the abortion industry can continue doing what they are doing?

3. Why do you think the abortion industry so industriously covers up any adverse affects abortion may have? How successful have they been in doing this?

6.9 Suggested Activities

1. View the documentary *Hush: A Liberating Conversation About Abortion and Women's Health*. What does this film tell us about the pro-choice movement? Why is it such

an important film?

2. Visit the Planned Parenthood website and read the sections on abortion and birth control. How effective is Planned Parenthood's marketing? Knowing what you now know, can you find any dishonest representations of a product or procedure?

3. Visit Live Action's abortionprocedures.com, and review the abortion procedures videos, as well as Lila Rose's interview with former abortionist Dr. Anthony Levatino. What information revealed here does the pro-choice movement most try to hide? What did you find most compelling about Dr. Levatino's transformation?

6.10 Additional Resources

- Live Action: abortionprocedures.com

  - The organization Live Action interviewed former abortionist Dr. Anthony Levatino and created a series of videos describing the abortion procedure. These videos do not include images of abortion victims, but powerfully explain how abortion procedures are done.

- Abortion Pill Reversal: https://www.physiciansforlife. ca/abortion-pill-reversal/

  - This article explains how the abortion pill can be reversed and the baby saved. It offers resources to help women in this situation, including a letter to your doctor that can be downloaded and printed.

- The Documentary — *Hush: A Liberating Conversation About Abortion and Women's Health*

  - This film, produced by a pro-choice woman, gives

compelling evidence for connections between breast cancer, pre-term birth and abortion.

- *Women's Health After Abortion: The Medical and Psychological Evidence,* by Elizabeth Ring-Cassidy and Ian Gentles.

  - This book is a great resource which explains in depth the affects an abortion can have on a woman's physical and mental health.

Part Seven: The Right Perspective

Truth without love is ineffective,
but love without truth is a lie.

"When we are no longer able to change a situation —
we are challenged to change ourselves."
Victor Frankl

7.1 Introduction

"What do you think about abortion?" I asked two teenage girls walking by.

"I don't think there's anything wrong with it," one of the girls replied. "At this point in my life, if I got pregnant I would have an abortion." Before I could ask a follow-up question, they turned and walked a few metres away, sitting down on the sidewalk to eat their lunches and watch other high-school students engage in conversation with my colleagues. They hadn't been hostile, but the girl's confidence in her decision to have an abortion if the situation arose disturbed me. This was a conversation opportunity I did not want to ignore. I walked over to them and asked, "Do you mind if I join you?"

They looked surprised. After hesitating for a moment, they both nodded. I sat down beside them.

"I'm Justina," I told them, reaching out to shake their hands.

"I'm Katelyn and this is Hannah." Hannah appeared most comfortable allowing Katelyn to do all the talking.

"Why do you think you'd have an abortion if you got pregnant?" I asked conversationally.

"Well, I'm super young," Katelyn replied. Hannah nodded in agreement. "Also," she added, "I couldn't raise a baby alone, and my parents would probably kick me out."

"Mine too," Hannah agreed.

We talked about **difficult circumstances** and the **humanity of the pre-born child**. Partway through our conversation, Katelyn stopped to survey me critically. "You know," she said finally, "you're different than a lot of people

I've talked to about abortion. You listen. I mean, you're sitting down on the pavement with us. I'm actually changing my mind now." By the end of the conversation, she said, "If I got pregnant I couldn't kill my baby. That would just be wrong." Hannah nodded emphatically in agreement.

They waved over a friend who had just come outside and he came to sit down beside us.

"What's all this about?" he asked me.

"Abortion," I told him. "What do you think about it?"

"What if a woman is raped?" he shot back. "It's got to be an option then."

Before I could reply, Katelyn jumped in. "Hey, hey!" she said quickly. "You don't have to kill the baby! Just place it for adoption!"

7.2 Being Good Ambassadors

When discussing controversial topics, it is important to remember that we are not only trying to win arguments, we are trying to win people. Gregory Koukl from Stand to Reason emphasizes the importance of being a good ambassador, an idea that is essential to being an effective pro-life advocate. No amount of logical reasoning can replace being kind and respectful. If the people we are engaging with do not feel that we respect *them*, they will have a difficult time believing that we respect *all* human beings in the way we say we do. Koukl points out that in order to be effective in conversations about important issues, we must have three characteristics: knowledge, wisdom, and character.[34]

---

34   Gregory Koukl, "The Ambassador Model," *Stand to Reason*, February 20, 2013, https://www.str.org/articles/the-ambassador-model#.WhbSb7YZO8o.

The first characteristic, knowledge, is essential. In starting a conversation about something as important as abortion, we must have at least a basic knowledge of how to defend our views. Having knowledge means that we understand what we have read in the previous chapters of this book and are aware of the different conversational tools at our disposal. However, the second and third characteristics are equally significant. Wisdom points to the fact that knowing what to say is only effective if we know how and when to say it, and character reminds us that we may talk the talk, but walking the walk is even more important.

Speaking to people about abortion can be difficult because of the effect it may have on us personally. Being an outspoken pro-life advocate means facing anger, scorn, and rejection, all of which can be tough to handle. Wisdom and character help us understand why it is so important to persevere. These characteristics enable us to utilize our knowledge effectively, so that we may change minds, and as a result, save lives.

7.3 Wisdom

A. How: A Soft Answer

Wisdom requires us to reflect on not just what to say, but how to say it. In discussing an issue as controversial as abortion, interactions are often tense, and can easily flare up. It is important that we prepare ourselves with how to respond wisely when we feel verbally attacked. In the Bible, Proverbs 15:1 tells us that: "A soft answer turneth away wrath: but grievous words stir up anger," and verse 2 declares: "The tongue of the wise useth knowledge aright . . ." Using our knowledge in a right way means that we do not use our words as weapons. When people convey their frustration with the pro-life position forcefully, it is often tempting to reply in kind. The question we need to ask ourselves is: *what will be achieved by doing so?*

The Book of Proverbs gives us the answer: if we rejoin frustration with frustration, people will become even more upset. If we are engaging in an angry debate, we are far less likely to adequately present the pro-life position, and a valuable opportunity will be lost. As difficult as it may be, wisdom requires us to answer furious accusations quietly and respectfully. It is surprising how people respond when they're angry and "You're a horrible person!" is answered by a polite: "Take care," or "Have a good day." Such an answer truly can "turn away wrath." It can be difficult to remember that, as hurt as we are at how we are treated simply for stating our beliefs, our focus cannot be on our own feelings. When we give a soft answer, we are more likely to engage even the angriest protestor in civil discussion, and these discussions may result in the saved life of a precious child.

B. When: Being Aware

In knowing how to convey the pro-life message in the most effective way, we must realize when we have received an opportunity to speak, and when we need to change the tone of our discussions. In conversation, listening to what someone is saying and how they are saying it is important, but we must also be aware of body language. When speaking with people, we receive both verbal and nonverbal cues, and understanding what these cues are telling us can be crucial. During certain conversations, it may appear as if the people we are speaking with are completely agreeing with us. However, at the same time they are shifting awkwardly, never making eye contact. Being in tune to body language can show us that we need to start asking different questions, and perhaps change the direction of a conversation.

One of the biggest indicators that the conversation needs to change direction is the revelation of a personal experience. Someone may tell us that they know someone who had an abortion, or that they were abused in the foster care system, or that they were sexually assaulted. When a personal experience is disclosed, we may need to drop our script of human rights and focus on what we are being told. If someone has been abused, we need to affirm their value as a human being. If someone tells us that they or someone they know has had an abortion, we need to offer sympathy for their loss and ask them how they are doing. If someone has revealed that they have been sexually assaulted, we need to ask them if they are safe. Wisdom tells us that we are not losing an opportunity to talk about abortion, we are gaining an opportunity to help someone through a difficult situation: an opportunity to prove that when we speak of the inherent dignity of all human beings, we are talking about the people in front of us, too.

Wisdom tells us when to speak and when to listen. In each interaction that we have, the goal should never be only to teach others. We should be focused on learning all we can from the people we are speaking with. There are times, however, when it is important that we speak up, and not allow ourselves to lose control over the conversation or be distracted from the issue we are talking about. The difficulty in emphasizing using discretion in conversation is that we are not born with wisdom. It is something that must be learned and at times, we will get it wrong. We have to be able to take criticism, both from fellow pro-life advocates and, if valid, from the people we are speaking with. Discussing sensitive topics is always a learning experience and recognizing that there is no such thing as a perfect conversation is ultimately what wisdom is all about.

7.4 Character

If our ultimate goal is to **make abortion unthinkable**, it is critical that we remember that "winning" an argument is not always how this will be achieved. In speaking out for pre-born children, we will often be accused of "shoving our beliefs down throats." It is imperative that we do not give this accusation any credence by answering back in anger, steamrolling another person's arguments, or behaving in a superior manner. If those we are speaking with feel antagonized, cornered, or patronized, they will be blinded to the truth we are presenting. Essentially, the truth is not presented by words alone. Being a good ambassador means that we must have a character that brings forward a winsome manner. While what we say is important, how we behave is often even more essential. Most people expect anyone advocating for the pro-life position to be pushy, demanding, and rude, as that is how the media has often portrayed the pro-life movement. Behaving in a way completely contrary to their expectations already calls their worldview into question in a considerable way. Long after people struggle to remember all that was said in a discussion, **they will remember how we treated them.**[35]

Essentially the character aspect of the ambassador model requires us to "practice what we preach." If we claim that all human beings are *deserving* of respect, then we ought to *treat* all human beings with respect, even if they stand in opposition to us. If we present the argument that we ought to help others rather than hurt them, then we must to be ready to provide any help that is necessary. Advocating the pro-life position is not enough: we must be willing to live out what that position entails. At times, this can be difficult, which is why our personal perspective can be so important.

---

35   This was emphasized to my fellow interns and I during intern training.

7.5 Finding the Right Perspective

Abortion is one of the—if not *the*—most controversial topics of our time. The statistics tell us that nearly 300 Canadian pre-born children are decapitated, dismembered, and disemboweled every single day. The actuality of 300 children necessitates the existence of 600 parents and 1,200 grandparents, not to mention the doctors, nurses, friends, and other relatives that are somehow involved in and/or affected by the abortion of these children. We live in a society where almost everyone has in some way been affected by abortion, and this reality means that abortion is deeply personal to countless people. Despite the claims of the pro-choice movement, many people have deep feelings of regret when it comes to their abortion, or perhaps anger at being caught in a situation where they felt that they needed one. Ultimately, there are many different feelings that bubble to the surface when abortion is mentioned, and most of those feelings are negative ones. In dealing with this negativity, we may lose valuable perspective.

When we are cursed at and called horrible names for claiming that human rights belong to all human beings, it can be hard not to take it personally. We may be tempted to yell back, and to defend ourselves from ad hominem attacks that take us away from talking about the issue at hand. When we feel rejected or attacked, we may fall back into the basic methods of fight or flight. Whenever this urge takes over, we must step back, take a deep breath, and ask ourselves the question: *Why?* Why is this person yelling? There is *always* a reason for a particular behaviour, and in this case, it is often true that those yelling the loudest on the outside are the ones crying the hardest on the inside. Someone may be yelling because their mother had complications while pregnant and her doctor told her to have an abortion. They may be upset because their aunt's pre-born child was terminally diagnosed, and she was told that having an abortion would end her child's suffering. Perhaps their sister was in an abusive situation and felt that abortion was her only option, or maybe they themselves have had an abortion. As the saying goes, "If you throw a rock into a group of dogs, the one that barks the loudest is the one that's been hit." When people are reacting in anger, we must not focus on how that personally makes us feel, but rather ask: Where is this anger coming from?

A. Responding to Ad Hominem Attacks

When people are angry and hurting, they often seek to distract from addressing the topic at hand—abortion. They do not want to address any abortion arguments, so they attack pro-life advocates in a personal way. (Ad hominem literally means "to the person" in Latin.) We may be called disgusting or told that we should be ashamed of ourselves. Name-calling is the most common ad hominem attack. In these cases, we must simply reply in a soft voice, attempting to draw them into conversation or wishing them a good day. However, there are some attacks that we should be aware of, so that we may respond effectively, and then once again refocus the conversation on the pre-born.

One of the common claims of the pro-choice movement is that pro-lifers only care about fetuses. "You pretend to care about people," someone might yell, "but as soon as a fetus is born you don't care what happens to it!" We can answer this accusation calmly, by stating: "We believe that *all* human beings have human rights, which means that we care about *every* human being. What I do or do not do to help other people has no bearing on the argument that killing innocent human beings is wrong." We may argue that we do help people and explain the ways in which we do, but ultimately, we cannot get distracted from our main focus. Whether we help born people may reflect on who we

Testimony Spotlight

"Hello, what do you think about abortion?" I asked a young woman walking by.

"I don't have an opinion on it one way or another," she replied.

We went through the human rights argument and spoke about difficult circumstances. She didn't disagree with anything that I had to say.

"So you agree that abortion is wrong?" I finished.

"Well . . . I really don't have an opinion," she answered.

I was confused, but thought there must be a reason why she didn't feel as if she could take a stance. "Do you know anyone who has had a personal experience with abortion?" I asked gently.

She hesitated. "My mom," she said finally. "She's had two abortions and a miscarriage."

"I'm so sorry that your mom went through that. How do you feel about it?"

"It's very sad that she had a miscarriage. I would have loved a sibling. But the abortions were her choice."

We spoke for a bit longer about the situation and how her mom is doing. By the end of the conversation she smiled at me and said, "You have given me a lot to think about. I'm going to share what you told me with my friends."

~ Caroline Slingerland

are as human beings, but it does not affect the moral status of the pre-born.

The claim that we don't care about born people often expresses itself as an accusation such as this: "Are you adopting children in need? Would you adopt a child?" Once again, whether we adopt children in need has no bearing on the truth of our arguments. In fact, many of us personally know people who have adopted children (if we have not done so ourselves), and further, most of us know couples who would love to adopt a child if they had the chance. The answer to this question differs according to the circumstances. Some of us may reply, "Absolutely! I would love to adopt a child in need, and if a woman was considering abortion I would certainly offer to parent her child." However, not all of us are in a position to adopt, and we may reply differently, "If a child was going to die unless I adopted him or her, I absolutely would do so. However, because I'm not in a social or financial position that best serves the interests of a child, I would recommend one of the many couples who have been adoption ready for years." If we know a couple who would like to adopt children, it is beneficial to mention their names as well, to prove that we do have contacts that enable us to help. After addressing their specific concern, we can refocus the conversation by saying: "However, imagine that I was not willing to adopt any children at all. How would my unwillingness to adopt a child give someone else the right to kill that child?"

People may also claim that we must not care about all the suffering in the world because we choose to focus on the issue of abortion. "What about poverty in Africa?" they might ask. "What about the homeless?" What they fail to recognize is that a focus on abortion does not mean that there is no understanding of other issues that need to be addressed. Rather, it is a recognition of the finite amount of time and energy people possess, and if we fight everything, we fight nothing. If we attempt to address every issue that we feel is important, we will be stretched thin and will be, for the most part, ineffective. Do we claim that doctors focusing on cancer research have no empathy for people suffering from tuberculosis? Do we accuse those working to end sex-trafficking of not caring for the struggling street children in Tanzania? There are many noble causes, and a focus on one does not negate interest in others.

Responding to personal attacks can be sensitive, and it can be hard not to be hurt or even to feel guilty, but it is important to focus on being *pro-active* rather than *reactive*. After responding to accusations calmly and rationally, we must seize the opportunity to refocus the conversation, maintaining our goal of helping the hurting to recognize the truth about abortion.

7.6 Giving the Right Perspective

When we have a healthy perspective personally, we can seek to help others change theirs. In talking about abortion, we often come into contact with people who are not ignorant of the pro-life position; rather, they are in denial. There are personal reasons why they find the pro-life position difficult to accept. In these cases, the apologetics that we have employed have fallen flat. The person we are speaking with may have agreed with the point we have made, and then moments later deny that same point. These conversations end up becoming circular, and often the person continually references one particular circumstance or issue. Once we recognize that logical reasoning is not being communicated effectively, we may need to change our focus. Instead of concentrating on apologetics geared towards head knowledge, we can turn to what we call **heart apologetics**. Heart apologetics employ tactics that we have already been using throughout our conversation, but with a slight change in direction. These tactics are to **understand**, to **love**, and to **inspire**.[36]

A. Understand

A famous prayer often attributed to Francis of Assisi[37] and widely circulated during the World Wars declares: "Let me not seek as much to be consoled as to console, to be understood as to understand . . ."[38] Seeking to understand is a fundamental part of being a pro-life ambassador. Without the willingness to listen to others, it is unlikely that a person will ever be won over to the pro-life position. People who have been affected personally by abortion are often suffering in ways we may or may not be able to understand. Without the desire to understand this suffering, we will lack the empathy needed to offer productive help. Seeking to understand emphasizes once again the importance of **common ground** and to acknowledge that certain circumstances seem impossible to overcome. It means asking **questions** and really listening to the answers. If someone realizes that we are interested in what they have to say, and that we are listening to their story and see them as a valuable individual, we have a foundation of kindness on which to build our conversation, rather than a foundation of distrust.

B. Love

In a sense, love is a word that defies definition. What most people can agree on is that love does not necessarily mean making someone else happy. Love, in essence, means

---

36   These three ideas were developed by Devorah Gilman.

37   Presented by Stephanie Gray in *Love Unleashes Life* (Toronto: Life Cycle Books, 2016), 13-14.

38   Jack Wintz, "A Closer Look at the Peace Prayer of Saint Francis," *Franciscan Media*, 2017, https://www.franciscanmedia.org/a-closer-look-at-the-peace-prayer-of-saint-francis/.

Testimony Spotlight

"I was raped." the young woman told me flatly. "I was drugged at a party while I was at university. I got pregnant. What was I supposed to do? I couldn't raise a kid on my own."

"I'm so sorry for your suffering," I said. "Are you comfortable with sharing more about your experience?"

"Yes, I don't mind."

"Who was there for you when you were going through this? Was anyone supporting your decision to have an abortion, or were there people who wanted to support you through the pregnancy?"

"I didn't tell anyone except my best friend, but she wasn't really comfortable talking about it. I know that there's supposed to be people you can talk to who will help you, but I didn't want to talk to all these people who would think that they could fix my life for me, assuming that they knew what I needed."

"If I was there during that time in your life," I asked carefully, "What could I have done to help you make a different decision?"

She thought for a moment before answering. "If you had just listened to me, let me tell you how I was feeling, I probably would have kept the baby. I didn't really want to have an abortion in the first place, I just felt so alone."

Testimony Spotlight - *continued*

I reached into my pocket and pulled out my business card. "If you or anyone else you know is ever in that situation, please call me. I won't tell you what you have to do, but I'll ask what it is that you need."

She took it and turned it over in her hand. After remaining silent for a moment, she said, "If you had been there, I wouldn't have had the abortion, and I know now that I'll never have another one."

~ Cameron Côté

wanting the best for the other, which, of course, does not mean that the other agrees with what one believes to be best. In our case, our mission is particularly difficult. Most people will feel that speaking out against abortion is the opposite of loving, and we will often be accused of having a lack of compassion. Loving others means speaking out anyway: speaking out for pre-born children to rescue them from death, and speaking out for women, explaining that there is *always* a better way than ending the life of a child.

For those of us in the pro-life movement, showing love manifests itself in a very practical way. It means that we speak when we want to remain silent, and it requires us to live by what we say. Love means directing post-abortive women to counselling and informing a high-school principle that a student is suicidal. It means reaching out to pregnant women who need help, making sure that we have their contact information so that we can connect them with pregnancy care centres and check in on them to see how they are doing. Loving those we speak to requires us to do the opposite of what pro-choice advocates claim that we do: follow up and follow through. Those in the pro-choice movement often claim that we care only about pre-born children, and that once women decide not to have an abortion we forget about both them and their children. Love requires us to be present as long as we are needed, and loving gives us the courage to do so.

C. Inspire

In working to change perspective, our goal must be to help people look outward instead of inward; to see the beauty in selflessness. So often in discussions about abortion, we may hear phrases such as: "But what about my career?", "I'm not ready to be a parent," or simply, "But what about *me*?" Parenting requires one of the highest levels of self-sacrifice, which is perhaps one of the reasons why many people are leaving parenting for later in life, or even outright rejecting it. However, one does not become a mother or father the moment their child is born; they become parents as soon as their child comes into existence at fertilization. Once we become parents, we are required to care for our offspring. This requires us to be unselfish.

One of the ways in which we can portray the importance of respecting a pre-born child's human rights even in inconvenient or difficult situations is by considering inspirational people.[39] We may point out that the people who inspire us are not those who took the easy road for the sake of personal comfort. Inspiring people are those who did the right thing, even though it was incredibly difficult. People such as Martin Luther King Jr. or Sophie Scholl are inspiring because they put their lives on the line to do what was right. We cannot say that

---

39   CCBR ran a blog series on inspirational people, illustrating that doing the right thing is often difficult.

216 | STUCK: A Complete Guide to Answering Tough Questions About Abortion

Testimony Spotlight

"What do you think about abortion?" I asked a young man.

"I think it's a necessary evil," he said, after considering my question for a moment. "I don't like it particularly, but there are difficult circumstances where it's necessary."

We talked about how all human beings should have human rights. He agreed but thought that an embryo or fetus was not worth as much as a more developed, born human being, particularly if they were going to be a strain on their parents and society. We talked about how we ought to rid society of problems rather than people.

"Shouldn't we give people the chance to rise above their situations?"

"Interesting point," he agreed, nodding. "I actually know someone like that. There's an amazing viola player in my class who came from Venezuela. He literally had nothing and grew up in poverty. A really bad situation all around, really. But he fought his way up and came to America. Now he's a successful musician."

"Would you still say, then, knowing what you know, that his mother should have had an abortion?"

"Of course not!"

Testimony Spotlight - *continued*

"Then how can we say that we shouldn't give all pre-born children the chance to overcome difficult circumstances in their life?"

We spoke for awhile longer about how doing the right thing is not always easy, but the result is inspiring.

"You're right," he said finally. "It's never okay to kill a human being, even if they're not born yet."

~ Jeremy Hooghiem

pregnancy and childbirth are easy, or that the choice between parenting and adoption is simple. Unplanned pregnancies can place people in extremely difficult situations. Doing the right thing in these circumstances may not be easy, but that does not change the fact that it is right.

Victor Frankl was a Holocaust survivor who wrote a powerful book about his experiences, *Man's Search for Meaning*. In this book Frankl details how concentration camps were filled with two types of people: saints and swine.[40] He came to realize that even when it appeared that everything was lost, there was something that the enemy could never take away. He wrote: ". . . everything can be taken from a man but one thing: the last of the human freedoms—to choose one's attitude in any given set of circumstances, to choose one's own way."[41] When faced with a difficult situation we cannot change reality, but we *can* change our perspective. Frankl used his insights to

---

40   Victor E. Frankl, *Man's Search For Meaning* (Boston: Beacon Press, 2006), 134.
41   Ibid., 66.

create a form of therapy, where he worked to change people's perception of their reality. He experienced great success, for, as he pointed out: "In some way, suffering ceases to be suffering at the moment it finds a meaning."[42] One particular pro-life campaign encapsulates the difficulty young parents face by telling the stories of mothers who choose life. Their stories do not declare that choosing life was easy, but they firmly state, "You'll never regret loving this much."[43]

7.7 Conclusion

Being faced with anger should not influence us to stop speaking the truth, though it should cause us to pause and reflect on why someone may be angry. If this person is angry because we treated them disrespectfully and without compassion, then how we are behaving is inexcusable. However, if they are angry because in presenting the pro-life position we have uncovered a tension that already existed deep inside of them, then we must continue speaking the truth. As Martin Luther King Jr. wrote in his letter from the Birmingham jail: "We who engage in non-violent direct action are not the creators of tension. We merely bring to the surface the hidden tension that is already alive. We bring it out in the open where it can be seen and dealt with."[44]

Good ambassadors speak out for the vulnerable knowledgeably, but they also do so with wisdom and character. Employing all three of these characteristics ensures that we will seek to understand the situation of those standing in front of us, and endeavor to inspire them to look beyond themselves to do what is right. Most

---

42   Victor E. Frankl, *Man's Search For Meaning* (Boston: Beacon Press, 2006), 113.

43   Darby, "Darby's Story," AbortioninCanada.ca, 2013, http:// abortionincanada.ca/youll-never-regret-loving-this-much/.

44   Martin L. King, "Letter from a Birmingham Jail," *University of Pennsylvania,* April 1963, https://www.africa.upenn.edu/Articles_Gen/Letter_Birmingham.html.

importantly, being a good ambassador requires us to love those with whom we speak. As Martin Luther King Jr. so eloquently said: **"Whom you would change, you must first love. And they must know that you love them."**

Key Takeaways

- To be effective pro-life ambassadors we need to communicate our knowledge with wisdom and have a winsome character.

- Wisdom: It is important to not just know what to say, but to know when and how to say it.

  - Speaking softly is important, as it deescalates a situation.

  - Knowing when to listen is just as important as knowing when to speak.

- Character: Long after someone has forgotten what we have said, they will remember how we treated them.

- How we view those we speak to is very important. Before answering in frustration, we need to ask why someone is upset. It is possible that someone has had a personal experience with abortion that causes them to lash out.

- In helping others find the right perspective we need to:

  - *Understand*

  - *Love*

  - *Inspire*

7.8 Diving Deeper

1. Has someone close to you ever done something wrong? How did/do you feel about it? Do you feel defensive? Why?

2. How would you feel if you met a woman who has had an abortion? What would you struggle with? Why is it so important to respond with compassion? How could your perspective influence this interaction?

3. Can you think of a time where you or someone else was betrayed by body language? How does your body react when you are in an uncomfortable position? What cues do you look for from others?

7.9 Suggested Activities

1. With a partner, practice discussing difficult situations. Do you respond differently when you know someone has been through something difficult? Together, write a list of possible questions you could ask in a sensitive conversation that are not confrontational.

2. Make a list of people who inspire you from both the past and the present. Why do they inspire you? What have they done that makes them worth looking up to?

3. In a small group, practice responding to ad hominem attacks. Discuss how they make you feel.

7.10 Additional Resources

- *Man's Search for Meaning,* by Victor Frankl

  - Victor Frankl's story of surviving the Holocaust is powerful, and the insights he provides throughout this book are invaluable.

- The Stand to Reason Website articles and videos on the ambassador model (*https://www.str.org/articles/the-ambassador-model#.XTcuhy0ZNsN*) (*https://www.str.org/about/ambassadors-creed*)

  - The Stand to Reason website offers great resources on how to connect with people and be an effective conversationalist, and explains what being a good ambassador for your beliefs looks like.

- *Love Unleashes Life*, by Stephanie Gray

  - This book discusses how to reach both the head and the heart of those you speak with, and offers powerful examples of real conversations.

Conclusion

*Sometimes it's easy to get caught up in the numbers and forget
that this is about real children. While I was doing
"Choice" Chain, a woman approached me and I asked her
what she thought about abortion. She then pointed to the little
brown-eyed boy in her stroller. She told me that little Noah was
alive because she saw what abortion was, and had a conversation
with one of CCBR's volunteers.*
~ Kerri-ann Brouwer

For many people, the word *abortion* is used as synonymous with "choice," "freedom," and "rights"—powerful words that are an essential part of a democratic society. But if each of the thousands of children who lose their lives every day had a face and a name, the word *abortion* would mean something entirely different to those who try to celebrate it. As tiny bodies are thrown into dumpsters and basement incinerators across North America, the question comes to each of us: *who will speak for them?* As Edmund Burke famously said, "The only thing necessary for the triumph of evil is for good men to do nothing." All it took to save baby Noah's life was a volunteer to gather her courage and start a conversation. This is something every one of us is capable of.

When we don't have to see the children who are lost, it can be easy to forget how important a conversation can be. It can be easy to let someone go with a laugh and a smile, "agreeing to disagree." But the stakes are too high for that. If we are wrong in our position, we are needlessly upsetting people and causing trauma to women. But if pro-choice advocates are wrong, thousands of human beings will continue to be torn apart under a cheerful banner of "personal freedom." We may agree *that* we disagree, and that both parties should continue to search for the truth, but we can never agree to accept that there are different positions on this issue.[1] We can never accept that there is a position that advocates the killing of innocents without standing up and speaking out.

It may be intimidating to voice our pro-life position, particularly in today's political climate, but hiding behind our fears and hoping someone else will step in and do what we are mandated to do is selfish. When we weigh our anxiety in the balance with the lives of precious children, how can we remain silent? The good news, for those of us reading

---

1   Stephanie Gray, *Love Unleashes Life* (Toronto: Life Cycle Books, 2016), 67.

this book, is that we do not have to be the trailblazers, and we are not alone. These arguments were developed by those who bravely took to the streets to defend the pro-life position, knowing the truth, but not necessarily knowing how to articulate it in a way that others would either accept or understand. We have the honour and privilege of standing on the shoulders of pro-life giants who went before us. They have placed in our hands solid apologetics, and now we have the responsibility to use them. As William Wilberforce said almost two centuries ago: "Let it not be said that I was silent when they needed me."

The lights begin to twinkle from the rocks:

The long day wanes: the slow moon climbs: the deep

Moans round with many voices.

. . . Come, my friends,

'Tis not too late to seek a newer world.

Lord Tennyson

Acknowledgements

To all of the great apologists who developed these arguments so that we could have the chance to use them.

To Jonathon—whose determined advocacy for pre-born children has ensured that I will forever be known as "Jonathon Van Maren's little sister." I couldn't be more proud of that; I wouldn't be here if it wasn't for you.

To Charmaine—who attempted to soothe the editing process with Oreo Iced Capps. The hours you spent analyzing every sentence of this book made it what it is.

To Charmaine—because you really deserve to be acknowledged more than once. This one is for the time you spent working out details. Discussing potential titles and covers. Hunting down illustrations. Offering moral support. Honestly, I think your name should be on the front of this book too.

To Auntie Elsie—who honestly told me when she didn't understand what I was getting at, and made sure that this book would have something for everyone.

To Maaike Rosendal, Blaise Alleyne, Stephanie Gray, and Kianna Owen for taking the time to give valuable feedback.

To my colleagues at the Canadian Centre for Bio-Ethical Reform—who dug through their lists of outreach stories to fill text boxes with testimony spotlights. You'll never know how many lives you were able to touch or how many babies were saved by the work you tirelessly do every day. Your courage and dedication is a constant inspiration.

To my husband, my parents, and my family for their unwavering belief in the importance of this work. Your support is invaluable.

To the supporters of the pro-life movement—your generous contributions enable pro-life activists to reach out to the culture and expose the horrific injustice of abortion. Your selfless giving has helped women choose life for their children.

To Sharon Grisnich, for the image and cover concepts and design. You understood what we needed when we weren't quite sure ourselves, and spent hours on it until we had the graphics we needed to express what this book is all about.

To Paul Broughton and the team at Life Cycle Books for working so hard to see this book in print. Thankyou, thankyou, thankyou.

Soli Deo Gloria.

About the Author

Justina Van Manen can't remember the first time she heard about abortion. With an older brother in the pro-life movement, abortion was something that her family discussed regularly. She began doing pro-life outreach at the age of fourteen, and continued volunteering with the Canadian Centre for Bio-Ethical Reform throughout high school.

During her first year of university, Justina went to Florida with CCBR's Abortion Awareness Project, which tours university campuses with a pro-life display. She was struck with how easy it was to effectively communicate the pro-life position to others, and the following summer she participated in CCBR's summer internship program. She continued her work with CCBR throughout university, graduating from Redeemer University with a Bachelor of Arts in English. She is currently working on a Bachelor in Education.

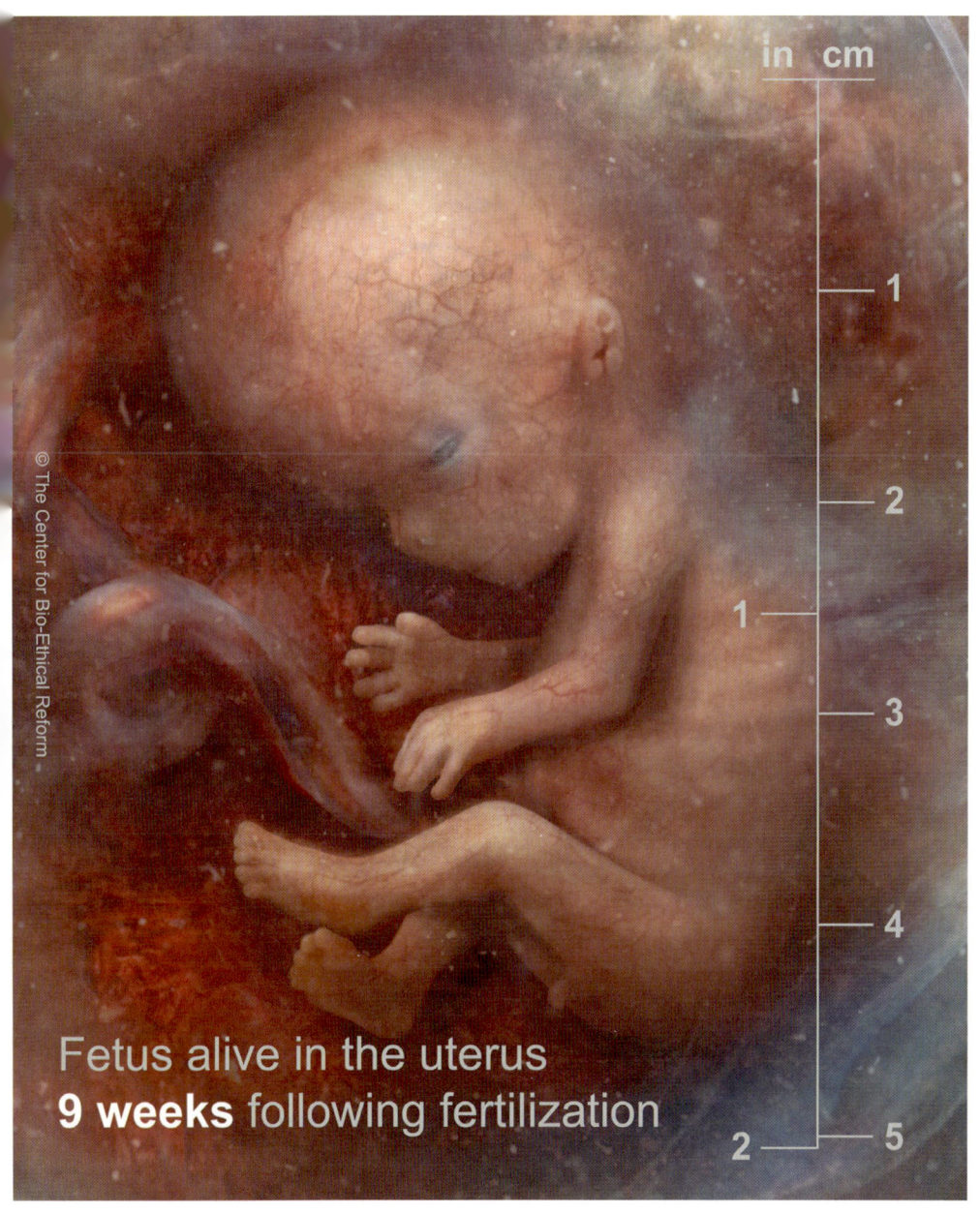

in cm

1

2

1

3

4

2   5

Fetus alive in the uterus
9 weeks following fertilization

This is a real in-utero photograph of a living 9-week fetus. We wished to place it in the book to show the humanity and beauty of the pre-born child. For the millions of children -just like this one- who have been aborted, we dedicate this to you.

Also from Life Cycle Books

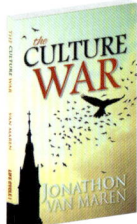

The Culture War
by Jonathon Van Maren

The Culture War examines the adverse effects of hook-up culture, pornography, abortion, euthanasia, and religious liberty from a Christian perspective. Written so that Christians can understand how we came to this cultural moment, and what we can do now that we are here. *240 pages, paperback. Also available as ebook on Amazon.*

#2261P

Seeing is Believing
Why Our Culture Must Face the Victims of Abortion
by Jonathon Van Maren

A powerful analysis of social reform movements and the timeless principles of exposing injustice. This hopeful book proves when the injustice of abortion is exposed, minds are changed and lives are saved. *176 pages, paperback. Also available as ebook on Amazon.*

#2265P

A Guide to Discussing Assisted Suicide
by Blaise Alleyne & Jonathon Van Maren

This thought provoking new book confronts the issue of assisted suicide head on, making the case that our duty to the suicidal is always to prevent the ultimate self harm of suicide. Practical, street-tested ways to change hearts and minds. *104 pages, paperback. Also available as ebook on Amazon.*

#2264P

Love Unleashes Life
by Stephanie Gray

Love Unleashes Life is a practical book designed to train readers how to have compelling and compassionate encounters when discussing abortion. Applying the methods of asking questions and telling stories, it engages and equips readers to provide a strong intellectual case for the pro-life message, as well as to reach those who have wounded hearts. *136 pages, paperback. Also available as ebook on Amazon.*

#2258P

www.lifecyclebooks.com